Praise fo.

We can never dwell too much on the grace of God. His grace is inexhaustibly rich and endlessly nourishing. And as Kyle DiRoberts reminds us in this book, grace is also a whole-Bible idea, gloriously manifest from the first pages of Genesis to the final words of Revelation. DiRoberts is a helpful guide on the journey, showing us the many faces and facets of grace across the pages of Scripture. Readers might go into this book humming the hymn "Amazing Grace," but they'll leave with a deeper appreciation of just how amazing grace is.

Brett McCracken, senior editor at The Gospel Coalition, author of *The Wisdom Pyramid: Feeding Your Soul in a Post-Truth World* and *Uncomfortable: The Awkward and Essential Challenge of Christian Community*

Christians gratefully affirm that salvation is by grace alone, but grace is much more than the basis of salvation. In fact, salvation of sinners is but one aspect of God's gracious and loving plan for His creation and merely the beginning of the impact of grace on believers. The Bible tells a remarkable story of the lengths and extent to which the Creator goes to defeat sin in all its forms. Death does not get the last word, grace does. Because of grace, believers live forever with the God who loves them in a new, redeemed creation where sin has been defeated and exiled. Writing in a style that invites the reader into conversation with the author, DiRoberts weaves together stories from the Scripture with those of his own experiences to unpack and illustrate the power of grace to transform those who embrace it. Readers will come to appreciate how amazing grace actually is.

Glenn R. Kreider, professor of Theological Studies, Dallas Theological Seminary

Grace Beyond Salvation is a must-read book that masterfully reveals the unbroken thread of grace woven throughout Scripture—from Genesis to Revelation—showing us that grace is not just a theme but the very heartbeat of God's redemptive plan. Reading this creative book will naturally deepen your love for the King and leave you in awe of His relentless, victorious grace. No matter the situation, grace always wins. Why? Because Jesus has already won!

Mark M. Yarbrough, President of the Dallas Theological Seminary

Oh, how we desperately need to understand grace and how it changes literally everything when we do! I am overjoyed in my heart thinking of how many people reading *Grace Beyond Salvation* will be freed from untrue guilt, shame, and false perspectives of ourselves and of God. Kyle DiRoberts uses Scripture and truth to breathe back grace, grace, grace to rejuvenate us into remembering how much we are loved and valued by God.

Dan Kimball, author of *How (Not) to Read the Bible*; Vice President of Western Seminary

KYLE DIROBERTS

Grace Beyond Salvation

REVEALING GOD'S LOVE FROM
GENESIS TO REVELATION

Moody Publishers

CHICAGO

Teresa Evenson Literary Agent, T.E.A.M. Services

Edited by Pamela Joy Pugh
Interior design: Ragont Design, Tammy Adelhardt
Cover design: Faceout Studio, Elisha Zepeda
Cover illustration by John Gould and Henry Constantine Richter (public domain)
Author photo: Austin Kehmeier

Library of Congress Cataloging-in-Publication Data

Names: DiRoberts, Kyle, author.
Title: Grace beyond salvation : revealing God's love from Genesis to
  Revelation / Kyle DiRoberts.
Description: Chicago : Moody Publishers, 2025. | Includes bibliographical
  references. | Summary: "From the first verse in the Bible to the very
  last, there's a thread that holds humanity's story together-that thread
  is grace. DiRoberts invites readers to understand and experience the
  biblical story of God's extraordinary grace. This story is the key to
  understanding and fully living our own stories"-- Provided by publisher.
Identifiers: LCCN 2025000301 (print) | LCCN 2025000302 (ebook) | ISBN
  9780802434746 (paperback) | ISBN 9780802470669 (ebook)
Subjects: LCSH: Grace (Theology)--Biblical teaching. | Bible--Criticism,
  interpretation, etc.
Classification: LCC BS680.G7 D57 2025 (print) | LCC BS680.G7 (ebook) |
  DDC 234--dc23/eng/20250220
LC record available at https://lccn.loc.gov/2025000301
LC ebook record available at https://lccn.loc.gov/2025000302

Originally delivered by fleets of horse-drawn wagons, the affordable paperbacks from D. L. Moody's publishing house resourced the church and served everyday people. Now, after more than 125 years of publishing and ministry, Moody Publishers' mission remains the same—even if our delivery systems have changed a bit. For more information on other books (and resources) created from a biblical perspective, go to www.moodypublishers.com or write to:

Moody Publishers
820 N. LaSalle Boulevard
Chicago, IL 60610

1 3 5 7 9 10 8 6 4 2

Printed in the United States of America

To Kaden, Oliver, and Carson. Life will not always go as planned. But may you always remember that His grace is enough. I love you.

To Lolly, you are my example of what it means to be gracious.
I love you.

Contents

The grace of the Lord Jesus be with all. Amen.

Revelation 22:21

Foreword

Have you ever had the sneaking suspicion that behind all the happy Christian talk of God's grace there lurks a sterner, less warmhearted God? What about what we see in the Old Testament, for example? Does a frowning Father hide behind Jesus the friend of sinners? So many Christians have this fear, that kindness is something that must be squeezed out of Him. It makes them slink away from Him in guilt, not daring to dream how good He is in truth.

Kyle DiRoberts parts such clouds for us by showing us that grace is not a strange one-off with the living God. Nor is grace just how God saves us. From the very beginning—before the universe even existed—He is a God who "longs to be gracious" (Isa. 30:18).

In this fresh and insightful book we get to see how the story of the Bible, from Genesis to Revelation, is the story of staggering and relentless grace. Walking through the Old Testament, we do not meet a harsh tyrant but One who could not bear the misery of His people, who longed to show them mercy, who delights in steadfast love. And on the story goes until the day He wipes all tears away. Here through the Bible we meet a God ready to forgive, full of pity, who loves us first before we ever love him. For He is the God who is love, a Father who has eternally loved His Son in the fellowship of the Spirit. Love for the other is central to His very being, so grace is not something strange for Him: He simply delights in mercy and kindness.

It all means that this book does something really quite unexpected. We might think that a more practical book, perhaps a self-help manual, would be the thing to improve our lives. "Give us some lifestyle advice!" we cry. Yet Kyle DiRoberts doesn't fall for that sort of thing. Instead, he takes our focus off ourselves. Now that may not sound good to you, because we really like thinking about ourselves! But as it turns out, reading this is like taking your eyes off your feet and getting a good look at the most glorious scenery. Kyle takes your focus and fixes it on the triune God in all the delicious beauty of His grace. And that, it turns out, is much more profoundly transformative than any self-help manual. Your very heart will be warmed in the sunshine of God's love.

So read on, behold our infinitely kind and unfailingly generous God, and your whole Christian life will brighten.

Michael Reeves
President and Professor of Theology,
Union School of Theology

CHAPTER 1

Roro

Did you have a lovey growing up?

Can't believe I'm starting this book with a story about a lovey.

Yes, I'm talking about that blanket or stuffed animal that went everywhere with you and brought comfort no matter where you were.

Did you have a name for your lovey?

In our family, it was always a big deal picking out just the right one. All three of our kids basically have the same style lovey. They are these really soft, somewhat small blankets, but what makes them unique is that they are themed differently.

Kaden's lovey is a dog named Roro.

Oliver's is an elephant named Snuffy.

And Carson has a cow named Lulu.

Most days end leaving Lolly and me exhausted. Especially on the weekends. As I write this, Kaden is eight, Oliver is six, and Carson is fifteen months old. Each weekend is filled with a basketball, football, or baseball game. Could be a golf tournament. Sometimes a birthday party. Perhaps dinner with friends or an event at school. Whoever came up with that expression "The days are long, but the years are short" is right. But we wouldn't have it any other way.

However, at the end of each day, there is still one last thing to do: put the boys to bed. This enterprise is something to behold. From downstairs it sounds more like a stampede of wild animals rushing back and forth than it does of anyone going to sleep. Lolly has this theory that the kids refuse to stop moving because they know they will pass out if they sit still for just a moment.

One of the most important events in our bedtime routine is trying to find each child's lovey. Good luck finding them, though—they could be anywhere. Lying on the chair at the kitchen table. On the floor in the bathroom. In one of the cars. Outside lying in the grass. Hidden in a golf bag. We have found lovies in the fridge. In the pantry. In between the couch cushions. Often, they are wrapped within another blanket or under the sheets. Throughout the day the kids could have gone anywhere, which means that lovey could have been left anywhere.

When it came time to pick out Oliver's and Carson's lovies, we had learned it was wise to buy two of the exact same one. This backup lovey is priceless when one goes missing. With the backup you can easily shout, "Look, here's Snuffy!" and resume looking for the real one later.

The Bedtime Score:

Parents = 1

Kids = 0

Bwahahaha (exhausted parent triumphant laugh)!

Another thing about lovies is that they wear out over the years. We noticed this first with Kaden because Roro was the oldest. As a result, Roro was tearing and beginning to unravel from all the abuse he had withstood over the years. On top of that, Roro's edges were significantly frayed. In some places Roro had holes, and as you could imagine Kaden wasn't helping keep the holes small either. On several occasions, Lolly has had to perform emergency surgery in order to sew Roro's head back on. Who knew being a parent meant you were signing up to be part surgeon?

Once we realized how nice it would be if Kaden had two lovies, Lolly went online to buy another one. But they didn't sell the same Roro anymore.

They had one that looked pretty close but wasn't exact. However, Lolly and I were desperate, so we bought the imposter and gave it a shot.

Then one night, after Kaden fell asleep, Lolly went in and kidnapped the "real" Roro so that she could wash him. I'll never forget the next morning. Kaden came out of his room with tears in his eyes.

"What happened to Roro?!"

He knew right away. He knew the feel. The smell. The touch. It wasn't the same. He knew it was different. It was as though the things that would cause you and me to question Roro's value were the very things that gave meaning to his relationship with Kaden.

At this point, you're probably thinking, what could a lovey possibly have to do with God's grace?

I'm not sure.

Just kidding.

What if Roro captured a glimpse of what grace was supposed to be like?

Not exactly, but close.

What if God's grace was not meant to be kept new or spotless? What if grace was meant to look as though it's barely holding it together?

And yet, grace will always hold everything together.

What if grace is meant to be bruised, filled with holes, frayed, and looking like it has been dragged through the mud of life?

What if grace is what keeps the Lord near to us at all times and nourishes us with confidence that God will never leave us nor forsake us? What if grace assures us that we are His and nothing can change that?

What if grace is meant to be bruised, filled with holes, frayed, and looking like it has been dragged through the mud of life? Yet unlike anything the world might offer, grace brings comfort and security and the durability to endure all that life might offer.

What if grace is never meant to be replaced with something else? What if there is no new and improved version of grace? Rather, it is the same grace yesterday, today, and tomorrow. Grace doesn't need to become anything different in order to meet us right where we are.

That's what this book is about. We are going to unravel the story of God's grace. The story as God revealed it to us through His Word. That from the beginning, God has never stopped or wavered in His desire to have a relationship with us.

For many, grace is understood almost exclusively as the means to our salvation. Ephesians 2:8–9 says, "*For by grace you have been saved* through faith. And this is not your own doing; it is the gift of God, not a result of works, so that no one may boast." Which is true and amazing and beautiful!

But grace is more tangled and messy and complex than that.

What we are going to discover is that grace is so much more than merely something that saves you. And as this book unfolds, we are going to witness a magnificent story about God's design and plan to dwell with us. A story that spans all of human history.

But this isn't just any kind of relationship.

We are talking about a relationship with God. Which means He is the one who determines what the relationship looks like. Not us. And for God, a relationship with Him looks like rest.

Rest?

Yes.

To some, rest is understood as a great night's sleep. Or it's having a slow weekend, maybe even a Sabbath day. Yet for others, rest is understood within the context of absence. The absence of pain and suffering and drama and trials and hardship in life.

However, for Christians, rest is different. Rest is not defined by the absence of those things; instead, rest is found as we are dwelling with God in the midst of the pain and suffering.

This reminds me of Psalm 23, when King David proclaimed, "The Lord is my shepherd; I shall not want. He makes me lie down in green pastures. He leads me beside still waters. He restores my soul. He leads me in paths of righteousness for his name's sake" (Ps. 23:1–3).

Right away we find restful language. In fact, the Hebrew word for "still" (*menuchah*, Ps. 23:2) can also be translated as "rest" or "resting place." Thus, the shepherd leads David, "beside restful waters."

But notice why David finds rest. It doesn't come from being in the green pastures; rather it comes from being with the shepherd.

Much later in the Bible, Jesus describes Himself as our good shepherd. He says, "I came that they may have life and have it abundantly. I am the good shepherd. The good shepherd lays down his life for the sheep" (John 10:10–11).

But back to Psalm 23, which takes a turn. It is no longer green pastures and restful waters. Now David describes enduring "the valley of the shadow of death." Yet even in the valley, David declares, "I will fear no evil" (v. 4).

This begs the question, "Why does he fear no evil?"

The answer is, "For you are with me" (Ps. 23:4).

In other words, we are rest*less* until we find God.

David finds comfort because he is dwelling with the shepherd.

Even in the valley, he finds rest because he has found the Lord.

> ### Where God is, rest is to be found.

As a result, David declares, "I shall dwell in the house of the LORD forever" (v. 6).

Having a relationship with God means that whether beside the green pastures or in the middle of the valley, God is with you.

Notice how God in Psalm 23 never promises that He will remove the hardship; instead, He promises to dwell with David throughout it. And where God is, rest is to be found. This is why a relationship with God is unlike any other relationship we could possibly have.

And it is grace that provides the sacred space for us to dwell with God at every moment of our lives.

As the story of God's grace is progressively revealed throughout this book, we'll discover a truth concerning grace that is going to provide the theological framework for our journey. That is, *God's grace was never intended to condone sin, but He did intend grace to endure our sinfulness, and triumph over it.*

Often, I wonder if there is some hesitation with exploring grace beyond our salvation due to a fear of what grace could potentially do left in the hands of sinners. For example, what if grace provided a Christian with an excuse that they can live however they'd like because there is grace and forgiveness to fall back on? One might even reference 1 John 1:9: "If we confess our sins, he is faithful and just to forgive us our sins and to cleanse us from all unrighteousness."

> God's grace was never intended to condone sin, but He did design grace to endure our sinfulness.

And yet, grace was never intended to condone sin.

In fact, right after John promises that God will forgive us, he says, "I am writing these things to you so that *you may not sin*" (1 John 2:1). For John, there was hope that confessing our sins would motivate us to not sin. That's why it's important we establish right from the beginning that God never intended grace for that purpose.

See, God's grace was never intended to condone sin, but He did design grace to endure our sinfulness. This confronts humanity with the unfortunate reality that we are sinful. Which means, even when we don't sin, we are still totally and completely depraved. Thus, we need grace not only to begin, but also to sustain our relationship with God long after we are saved.

For some (even many biblical characters!), grace enduring one's sinfulness bothers them. If I'm honest, writing this book has revealed how much it disturbs me too. But what if, once we honestly embrace how sin and our sin nature has affected our relationship with God, the more beautiful and amazing and humbling the grace of God becomes?

Moreover, there is no greater example of God's grace enduring our sinfulness than the passion of Christ. When Jesus willingly underwent His gruesome death on the cross to save us. It was at the hands of sinners where Jesus was abused in order to save sinners and provide an everlasting, eternal, forever, never-ceasing relationship with God.

God's purpose for His grace is that it would withstand our sinfulness so that we might dwell with God. And here's the thing: This is how *God* intended grace.

Not us.

In fact, God has never asked us how or when we would like to receive grace. He has never asked us about who He should extend grace to.

This is His sovereign decision. His providential plan.

That's why it is important that you hang in there with me, because it's going to take our entire journey to awaken to what this phrase actually means. That said, don't feel any pressure to understand it all now. Or maybe, try to resist any urge to fill in what you think it *might* mean. Instead, let's walk through this together as the Lord patiently reveals the grace of the Lord Jesus to us.

Part One—Grace Before the Fall

This section looks to Adam and Eve and their life with God prior to the Fall and the way things were supposed to be. What we learn is going to reveal a side of grace that has not been affected by any of the events to follow after Adam and Eve ate from the tree of the knowledge of good and evil. In this light, grace can be hard to envision because we live in a world still totally and completely affected by the Fall. But before everything changes, we will do our best to enjoy what grace reveals about humanity's relationship with God.

Part Two—Grace After the Fall

Everything changes after Genesis 3:6. One way to think about this time period is that things are now not the way they were supposed to be. Grace doesn't encourage sin, but in light of the Fall, in order to have a relationship with God we will discover that grace has this supernatural ability to endure our sinfulness. Not to promote or celebrate, but rather to withstand for the purpose that we might dwell with God. This ministry of grace cascades throughout almost the entire Bible. Through it all, it is grace that enables, fosters, and sustains how we dwell with God.

Part Three—Grace in the New Heaven and New Earth

In the end, it's the grace of the Lord Jesus that restores all things to the way they were meant to be. This section considers life with Jesus in the new heaven and new earth. A time when death and sin are finished. It is done. When grace triumphs over sin. This is the period of time in which we will receive our glorified bodies and when, once again, we will be at rest with God, but now for an uninterrupted eternity. These will be sacred and holy moments shared with Jesus, a relationship that only grace can create.

If you are up for it, I would like to invite you along with me as we travel through many amazing stories in the Bible. We will meet the first man and woman to ever live. We will spend time with God's beloved prophet. We will step into some interesting family drama. And meet Jesus in His most vulnerable moments. We will also peer into the future and what things will be like then—things like the new heaven and new earth, and the resurrection and what it all means for us.

Here is what's so astonishing: For our relationship with God to exist, we are going to discover that it must be rooted and grounded in His grace. And there has never been a time when this wasn't true.

One more thing. I'm not writing from a place of completion as it relates to grace.

No.

My relationship with God needs grace today just as much as anyone. My soul longs to rest with its Shepherd. That said, even though I am providing the direction for us on this journey, please know I am taking you somewhere I'm familiar with. And it's a safe and loving and hopeful place. It's a place where God is. And where God can be found. It's where a relationship with God exists.

I still can't believe I started this book with a story about a lovey.

PART ONE

Grace
Before
the Fall

Introduction to Part One

Have you ever wondered what it was like to dwell with God in the garden prior to the Fall?

When no one had been affected by sin or sin nature.

When death wasn't a reality to our human experience.

When sickness wasn't even a thing yet.

When humanity felt no brokenness toward one another.

When pain and sadness hadn't been felt.

When a relationship with God had no interruption.

We can go back to that time.

It's found right at the beginning of the Bible. But I offer this caution. These few chapters will leave us wanting. And in some cases, the Bible will leave us with more questions than answers. But I'm beginning to think that's on purpose, especially when our subject matter is God.

However, what we *will* find is grace. What we will find is that God graciously brings forth everything. God even creates this unique kind of creature in His image.

Everything was good—in fact, it was very good.

It was perfect, complete, lacking in nothing because creation was at rest dwelling with God. And because God has no beginning and no end, the relationship God shared with His creation was meant to last forever.

Grace makes forever possible.

Part One moves from Genesis 1:1 to Genesis 3:5, but hold on, because it goes quickly. Then, everything changes in Genesis 3:6.

Well, everything changes except God.

God never changes. Which means, grace never changes.

Here's my hope, that by the end of Part One you find yourself longing for this kind of relationship again.

CHAPTER 2

From Beginning to End

Kaden has been learning how to read, and just the other day he asked, "Daddy, do you want me to read to you the very first verse in the Bible?"

I said, "Of course! I would love that." Then I added, "It is one of my favorite verses!"

Kaden then opened his Bible and found Genesis 1:1 and began to read. Well actually, before he started, he made sure I was paying full attention. Then, with his sweet but growing voice, he read, "In the beginning, God created the heavens and the earth."

Once he finished, he looked up to see what I thought. Then I did one of those dad things where you whisper and yell at the same time, I said, "Good job, buddy! I'm so proud of you! You read that great!"

But I also had a question. "Who is God? It sounds like from this verse that God is the Creator of everything. So, who is this God?"

This is when my kids regret that their dad is a theology professor.

Kaden hesitantly suggested, "God is the Trinity?"

I said, "Great! But what's the Trinity?"

He said, "There is one God and God is three persons."

Then I asked, "Who are the persons?"

He said, "The Father, the Son, and the Holy Spirit."

I said, "That's awesome, dude!"

Then I looked at him with a fun, but pondering face. "Hmm, let's go back to Genesis 1:1, when it said, 'In the beginning, God created . . .'" I pointed to the words "God created" and asked, "Who is doing the creating? Was it the Trinity or one of the persons of the Trinity, like the Father, or the Son, or the Holy Spirit?"

He thought for a moment and said, "I don't know. Maybe the Trinity. Maybe the Father. I don't know. Who was it?"

My response was no longer puzzlement, but I announced: "Jesus."

Kaden then looked at me as though he wasn't too sure about that. But he simply said, "Huh."

Then I asked, "Buddy, since you read Genesis 1:1, can I read you a verse or two from Colossians?"

He said, "Sure!"

Together we made a beeline to the far right of the Bible, passing through many pages and words and verses and chapters and books to finally arrive at Colossians 1:15–17. There I began to read, "He is the image of the invisible God, the firstborn of all creation" (v. 15).

Then I quickly stopped and asked, "Who do you think the 'he' is from Colossians 1:15?"

Kaden thought for a moment, and said, "Jesus!"

I said, "Yes."

Then I asked Kaden if it would be all right if I read the passage again, but this time I would replace "he" or "him" with "Jesus" because that's who Paul is talking about.

He said, "Sure!"

Then I read Colossians 1:15–17 like this: "Jesus is the image of the invisible God, the firstborn of all creation. For by Jesus all things were created, in heaven and on earth, visible and invisible, whether thrones or dominions or rulers or authorities—all things were created through Jesus and for Jesus. And Jesus is before all things, and in Jesus all things hold together."

I looked up, "See bubba, in Genesis 1:1 it says, 'In the beginning, God created the *heavens and the earth.*' And in Colossians 1:16 it says, 'For by Jesus all things were created, in *heaven and on earth.*' It's Jesus. Isn't that crazy?"

Kaden said, "That's cool!"

Then I explained, "That's why I thought of Jesus when you awesomely read to me Genesis 1:1."

Then he smiled.

And his smile was one of those smiles as though I had just told him something really cool and he wanted to go tell his little brother, but of course he was going to explain it to Oliver as though he thought of it himself.

It makes sense that someone might read "In the beginning, God created the heavens and the earth" and think that this is the Trinity, or if it was a particular person of the Trinity, then it would likely be the Father. I think when most people read the word "God" in the Bible, especially in the Old Testament, they assume it is talking about the Father.

To make it even more complicated, Moses, the guy who wrote Genesis, likely did not have a perfect understanding about Jesus' role in creation. He may not have known that Genesis 1:1 was referring to Jesus or to any person of the Trinity. To Moses, "In the beginning, God created" simply meant that God (*Elohim*) was the Creator.

And that's okay.

But it's also okay for us to see Jesus too.

When reading the Bible, it is quite normal for other verses or passages or stories to help make sense of another verse or passage or story—even if that verse or passage or story is in a completely different book of the Bible. Perhaps even separated by hundreds or thousands of pages.

In a real way, Kaden knows more about Genesis 1:1 than Moses did.

Wait, what?

How?

Because Kaden has the whole Bible to lean on, whereas Moses didn't. Kaden is able to read the New Testament, but Moses couldn't. It didn't exist yet.

It isn't until we get all the way to the New Testament that we learn more about how Genesis 1:1 unfolded. And what we find in Colossians 1:15–17 is the One behind the creation of everything.

It's Jesus.

Now, surely some of you are still on the fence. Still not convinced that Genesis 1:1 is about Jesus.

Let's look at one more example.

For this, we'll go to the gospel of John.

There we find a scene in which the Jewish religious leaders are seeking to kill Jesus.

This sounds intense.

Why did they want to do that?

When Jesus references the "Scriptures," He is talking about the Hebrew Bible. The Old Testament.

Because Jesus was claiming equality with God (John 5:18).

In the middle of John 5 we read an exchange between Jesus and the religious leaders, and Jesus doesn't back down. He tells them that only the Son of God has the authority to grant eternal life (v. 24).

And to demonstrate that he has this kind of authority Jesus appeals to "another who bears witness" about Him (v. 32).

Who is this person?

Immediately, Jesus mentions John the Baptist and the testimony they received from him. Which was a big deal in itself. But that isn't who Jesus has in mind. He has someone *greater* than John in mind (v. 36).

Jesus then gives a little hint. He tells them, "You search the Scriptures because you think that in them you have eternal life; and it is they that bear witness about me" (v. 39).

Search the Scriptures?

When you and I think of the word "Scriptures," we think of the whole Bible . . . containing both the Old and New Testaments. But at this time, the Bible as we know it today didn't exist. The New Testament hadn't been written. That means when Jesus references the "Scriptures," He is talking about the Hebrew Bible. The Old Testament.

And according to Jesus, the Scriptures (i.e., Old Testament) bear witness "about me" (v. 39).

By the way, where is Genesis located?

The New or Old Testament?

Then Jesus continues, He gets more specific.

Jesus says, "There is one who accuses you: Moses, on whom you have set your hope. For if you believed Moses, you would believe me; for he [Moses] wrote of me" (John 5:45–47).

Moses is the greater witness.

Greater than even John the Baptist.

Who wrote Genesis 1:1? Moses.

And who does He say Moses was writing about? "Me."

Well, not me, as in Kyle. But "me," meaning Jesus (John 5:46).

Do you know how startling of a claim this would have been to the Jewish religious leaders? This is why they wanted to kill Him. Jesus in John 5 is claiming equality with God and to be the very subject matter of the Scriptures.

Let's go back to Paul in Colossians.

What Paul is doing in Colossians 1:15–17 is understanding the Scriptures like Jesus did. Paul is reading Moses' words in Genesis and believes they are about Jesus. Thus, he concludes that "by him [Jesus] all things were created, in heaven and on earth" (Col. 1:16).

By the way, Colossians says something else about Jesus' authority as Creator that I didn't bring up to Kaden that day. Paul writes in Colossians 1:17, "And he [Jesus] is before all things, and in him [Jesus] all things hold together."

Hold together?

In the Greek, "hold together" (*sunestēken*) carries with it the idea that something has been brought into existence. That makes sense because in Colossians 1:15–16 it was Jesus who is responsible for creation. However, what Paul doesn't want us to miss is how Jesus is also the one sustaining and holding creation together.

Another place in the Bible mentions this. It's in a book called Hebrews, and the author describes Jesus like this: "He [Jesus] is the radiance of the glory of God and the exact imprint of his nature, and he upholds the universe by the word of his power" (Heb. 1:3).

Jesus upholds what?

Oh, you know, just the universe.

In the Greek, "uphold" (*pherōn*) means to hold something in a continued state of existence.

The consequence here is that if Jesus weren't to uphold the universe, it would at best spiral out of control. And at worst would cease to exist. Even to this moment, that is how dependent creation is on its Creator. Creation, with its breathtaking beauty and awe-inspiring complexities, was never intended to be self-sufficient for its existence.

Let's go to the gospel of Matthew for a moment—there we find Jesus in a boat with His disciples. Matthew describes the scene like this: "There arose a great storm on the sea, so that the boat was being swamped by the waves" (Matt. 8:24). As a result of the storm, the disciples are terrified because they think they are going to die.

Where is Jesus?

Isn't God Himself dwelling with them in the boat?

Yes, but Matthew describes how Jesus was sleeping in the boat. Imagine that, in the midst of the disciples' fear of dying, Jesus is snoozing away.

I wonder if He snored.

Then the disciples wake Jesus up and beg for help. "Save us, Lord; we are perishing" (v. 25). To which Jesus replies, "Why are you afraid, O you of little faith?" (v. 26).

What happens next is unforgettable. Jesus gets up and rebukes "the winds and the sea" and as a result "there was a great calm" (v. 26).

Now I always used to read that and think this makes sense because Jesus is God. And that is something God would do. God would have the kind of authority to tell a storm to be quiet.

Which is true. However, I think there is more going on.

Colossians 1:15–17 and Hebrews 1:3 reveal that Jesus is not only the Creator, but that He is also the Sustainer of everything. Even the one who holds everything together with the power of His word. That means when the storm calms down in Matthew 8:26, it isn't enough to say that the storm was merely listening to God. Rather, what the storm was doing was listening to its Creator *and* Sustainer. The storm was listening to the One holding all things together.

Thus, when your Creator and Sustainer commands you to calm down, what do you do?

You calm down.

Let's go back to where we started from in Genesis 1:1, and the idea that "in the beginning, God created the heavens and the earth." Not only is this verse about Jesus, but I also think this verse contains the very first instance of grace in the Bible.

Grace?

Yes.

But how? Genesis 1:1 doesn't mention the word grace.

This is true. It doesn't mention the name Jesus either.

Grace is present because what God does in Genesis 1:1 *is* gracious.

How is it gracious?

Because when God creates something, this is a gracious thing to do. Nothing in creation did anything to deserve its existence. And it doesn't take but five words in the Bible for God to reveal His grace, that "In the beginning God *created*" (Gen. 1:1).

Then in order to further reveal the gracious nature of creation, the Bible describes how it was God's plan all along to give all that He has created to mankind to rule and have dominion over (Gen. 1:26–27).

This is quite a gift.

This is grace.

And in the coming chapters, we are going to consider the various ways God graciously brought forth creation. For now, my hope is that we can rest in the wonder and amazement that the very first verse in the Bible reveals God's gracious initiative to have a relationship with us. A plan that began with Jesus and grace.

Thus, "In the beginning, God [Jesus] created [grace] the heavens and the earth" (Gen. 1:1).

I wonder how the Bible ends. Can you imagine if the Bible ended the same way it began, talking about Jesus and grace?

You ready?

The very last verse of the Bible says, "The grace of the Lord Jesus be with all. Amen" (Rev. 22:21).

And just like that the Bible is finished.

But before it ends, it concludes with what?

Grace.

The grace of who?

The Lord Jesus.

And who is the grace of the Lord Jesus meant for?

All.

"The grace of the Lord Jesus be with all. Amen."

The same Jesus who began the Bible concludes the Bible.

The same grace who provided everything for us to dwell with God in the beginning is the same grace that will provide all we need to have a relationship with God in the end. And really there is no end to a relationship with God. We are meant to dwell with God forever. Which means there is no end to grace either.

From the beginning to the end, it is the grace of the Lord Jesus.

What was originally hidden in Genesis 1:1 is now revealed through the person and work of Christ. There is no greater example of grace than God giving Himself to us at each stage of redemptive history so that we might dwell with Him.

The biblical story is one in which we continue to learn that we are His and He is ours. That the thread that unifies the Bible from start to finish is the unbroken, uninterrupted, ceaseless, sustaining, permanent, unblemished, perfect grace of the Lord Jesus.

This just might be the greatest love story ever told.

It is a gracious story about dwelling with Jesus.

CHAPTER 3

Everything

With the very first verse of the Bible, we are supernaturally and mysteriously introduced to the grace of the Lord Jesus. Even more, all that Jesus creates reveals God's gracious plan for humanity. A plan in which He intends to dwell with us forever.

But what does Jesus actually create?

Everything.

But what does *everything* even mean?

This is what we end up discovering in the verses after Genesis 1:1.

For example, on the first day Jesus created light, which separated the light from the darkness (Gen. 1:4). God called "the light Day, and the darkness he called Night" (v. 5).

On the second day Jesus created what is described as "an expanse in the midst of the waters" so that it would "separate the waters from the waters" (v. 6). The Bible describes how "God called the expanse Heaven" (v. 8), or the "sky," or "the heavens."

Then, on the third day, Jesus gathered the waters under the heavens into one place and He created dry land (v. 9). He called the dry land Earth and the gathered waters he called Seas (v. 10). Then Jesus created vegetation, plants, and fruit trees (v. 11). The Bible also describes that the plants and fruit trees yielded seed, which would then bring forth more plants and more fruit trees to help nourish the earth (v. 12). This day ends with "And God saw that it was good" (v. 12).

On the fourth day Jesus created the sun and the moon and the stars (v. 16). These large and beautiful luminous objects were to give light to the earth (v. 17) and help in determining seasons, days, and years (v. 14). This day similarly ends with, "And God saw that it was good" (v. 18).

Then on the fifth day Jesus created from within the "waters" swarms of living creatures (v. 20). So far, I've been fine. But now all I can think of is sharks. Did anyone else growing up get a little nervous swimming in a pool at night? You know, in case somehow a shark got in there when no one was looking. No? Just me?

Jesus then creates birds, which would fly above the earth and fly "across the expanse of the heavens" (v. 20). Also on the fifth day, God offers for the first time a verbal command to something He has created: "Be fruitful and multiply and fill the waters in the seas, and let birds multiply on the earth" (v. 22). Then on the fifth day Jesus created all living creatures on the earth; this included livestock, creeping things, and beasts of the earth (v. 25).

Overall, it sounds like the fifth day wants to hurt me. I mean, creeping things and swarms of living creatures in the ocean and beasts? Nevertheless, this day ends with, "And God saw that it was good" (v. 25).

By the time we get to Genesis 1:25, the first five days are complete. Then on the sixth day mankind is created. And in the following chapters we talk a lot more about this.

There is one aspect of creation we need to discuss for a moment. A lot of people have different opinions about Genesis 1 and particularly the days of creation.

Some people believe the earth is quite young. Others believe the age of the earth is rather old. For many, it is an issue they are passionate about, and the controversy rests on whether each day of creation was one twenty-four-hour period or if each day represented millions or even billions of years.

Maybe you're thinking, "I had no idea! I never thought of that before!" And that is totally fine. An answer (or lack thereof) doesn't affect where we are going at all. For now, I suggest that there are brilliant, science-affirming Christ-following men and women who have different opinions on the meaning of the various days of creation.

So why bring it up?

Because I wanted to at least acknowledge the elephant in the room. But with that said, I'd also like to ask for permission to leave the elephant alone for now.

Will you trust me on this?

Instead, this is what I'm hoping we will come to appreciate about creation (Gen. 1:1–25). So far, the entire first chapter of the Bible has been about Jesus creating everything. And what Jesus creates is good. In fact, creation has a gracious formula: There was nothing and then there was something and it was good.

Have you ever heard a Christian use the expression "by the grace of God" to describe a way in which God has provided for them? Have you ever said this yourself?

The examples of how one might use this expression is limitless. Which makes sense because God is limitless. It also means so are the ways God can lavish His grace on us.

> Our lives tell creation-like stories all the time.

It could be as simple as thinking you are going to run out of gas because you have been driving on empty for so long, yet *by the grace of God* you make it to the gas station just in time. It could be something more serious, like maybe you've lost your job and need work or else you could lose your house or car or perhaps can't feed your family. Yet *by the grace of God* you find a job that covers your expenses so that you can provide for your family. Maybe it is a medical issue, and perhaps you have been suffering for years with a chronic illness and have had no relief. Yet *by the grace of God* a doctor has finally found a remedy that is providing relief.

You might be thinking, "But what in the world does this have to do with the creation account from Genesis 1?"

I'm glad you asked.

I think our lives tell creation-like stories all the time.

In fact, each time we proclaim "by the grace of God," what we are professing is a distinct Christian reality concerning God's grace. That when there was nothing, He provides something, leaving the Christian to confess, "By the grace of God."

However, what professing "by the grace of God" doesn't mean is that we have experienced some kind of spiritual luck. As though we have really dodged something bad and since Christians don't believe in luck, we simply affirm, "By the grace of God."

That's not grace.

God's grace has nothing to do with karma either. We didn't get to the gas station just in time because we helped out a friend earlier and God is just paying it forward by making sure we don't run out of gas.

That's not how grace works.

There is no such thing as luck based on what we know about the grace of the Lord Jesus in creation. Creation is not random. It is intelligent. It is designed. It has a plan. It is thoughtful, and everything has purpose. As the Creator and Sustainer, Christ graciously provided when there was nothing. Which then shouldn't be that shocking when even now God continues to provide when all hope is lost. When we feel as though there is nothing.

And let's be clear, it isn't *only* those instances in which we receive something that we then validate the reality that it is "by the grace of God." Technically, *everything* is by the grace of God. It is just sometimes we are graciously made aware of it. Remember when we talked about Jesus not only being the Creator, but that He also holds all things together by the power of His word (Heb. 1:3)? From our human perspective we don't see all that God upholds, even though He is holding *everything* together.

And how is this possible?

Yep.

By the grace of God.

How about the next time we find ourselves using the expression "by the grace of God," or hear someone else proclaim such powerful words, we remember all the way back to Genesis 1? That with the Creator it is quite normative for God to provide when there is nothing. It is those creation-like moments that draw us near to the Lord.

When there is nothing, He provides something.

This is how the grace of God works.

Grace always seems to reveal itself when we have nothing left.

CHAPTER 4

Hummingbirds

Not too long ago I began to notice on my phone a bunch of photos I didn't take. They were beautiful and I was confused. Where did they come from? There were a number of photos of birds flying in the air. One in particular caught my eye—it was a hummingbird in mid-flight.

Who captures a hummingbird like that?

This immediately brought me back to God's command in creation that the birds were to fly across the expanse of the heavens (Gen. 1:20). Someone had taken my phone and photographed God's command on the fifth day of creation, and I wanted to know who.

I asked Lolly if she had taken the photos and she said, "No, not me."

Then I asked the boys.

To which Oliver said, "Why, Daddy?"

I said, "Because there are a bunch of photos on here that I didn't take."

Then Oliver quietly said, "I took them Daddy, I'm sorry. I just love taking pictures."

I said eagerly, "*You* took them?"

He then looked at me as though, *This isn't going how I thought it would.*

I said, "Buddy, those are incredible!"

Then I asked him, "You know who else loves to take photos?"

He said, "Who?"

I pointed at myself and said, "Me, buddy."

In fact, I can still remember as a little boy when I noticed something beautiful, I'd close my eyes and then quickly open them as though my eyes were built-in cameras.

Then I proposed to Oliver, "We should go take photos together. Wouldn't that be fun? Would you like that?"

To which he smiled and nodded his head in agreement while raising his eyebrows up and down.

To this point, we've looked at the first five days of creation. And even though Jesus has been doing the creating, the Trinity has been present the whole time.

The sixth day of creation is a little different. On the sixth day the Bible mentions the direct involvement of the Trinity, the Bible says, "Let *us* make man in *our* image, after *our* likeness" (Gen. 1:26).

However, the Bible never tells us the numerical value of "us" or "our" from Genesis 1:26, but we know from church history and the rest of the Bible that God is one being, eternally existent as three persons—the Father, Son, and Holy Spirit.

Something else the Bible reveals is that for the first time in creation something is graciously created in God's image. For the first time we have someone, not just something. And the someone is Adam and Eve.

After God creates Adam and Eve there is a command, which isn't legal in nature. It is grounded by an enjoyment of who God is and what He has just spent the last five days doing. The command is, "Be fruitful and multiply and fill the earth and subdue it, and have dominion over the fish of the sea and over the birds of the heavens and over every living thing that moves on the earth" (v. 28).

God's creation is a gift to mankind, and they are meant to enjoy it, and to enjoy means to do things like fill and subdue and have dominion over the earth.

Hold on; "subdue" and "dominion" don't quite sound like the most loving or endearing characteristics one could embody. In fact, subdue means to lord over or be the master of something. In this case, Adam and Eve are meant to lord over creation. That just sounds weird. In addition, to have dominion means to rule over something, and that means Adam and Eve are to rule over God's creation.

But who has ever enjoyed being ruled, or lorded over, by someone else?

What if there was something going on with Genesis 1:28 that would cause these words to have a different meaning than what we're familiar with?

Here's what I'm thinking.

In Genesis 1:28 the words "subdue" and "dominion" haven't been affected by sin nature yet. The Fall hasn't occurred yet. Which means, Adam and Eve are perfectly exercising their God-given authority over creation. In other words, "subdue" and "dominion" have never been used to hurt or abuse anyone or anything within creation. Thus, in Genesis 1, to subdue or have dominion is understood in a positive and good and holy way.

Then Genesis 1 goes on to explain that Adam and Eve have been given "every plant yielding seed that is on the face of all the earth, and every tree with seed in its fruit. You shall have them for food" (v. 29). This verse is interesting, especially when you read it together with Genesis 2:9.

> We don't find God merely filling our bellies, but food in the garden is described as pleasant and beautiful and joyful and precious and delightful.

You might be thinking, why would we jump to Genesis 2 when we aren't done with Genesis 1 yet?

Because in Genesis 2 we learn a little more about what creation was like in those six days in Genesis 1. And in Genesis 2:9 the Bible describes creation this way: "And out of the ground the LORD God made to spring up every tree that is pleasant to the sight and good for food." Notice the way trees are described. Trees are not brought forth merely to do a job.

They are created to be enjoyed. They are created to be looked upon. They're meant to be aesthetically pleasing to the sight.

You might ask, "What makes you think that?"

Notice how the Bible describes the trees as "pleasant to the sight." What God creates is not only practical in nature, but it's beautiful. Even something to be desired.

And food, what about food? As an Italian I strongly believe that it isn't good enough to just fill your belly. Italians want food that tastes good. Smells good. Looks good. In Genesis 2:9 we don't find God merely filling our bellies, but food is described as delectable, given to be enjoyed.

Again, one might ask, "What makes you think that?"

The Bible says, "And out of the ground the LORD God made to spring up every tree that is pleasant to the sight and good for food" (Gen. 2:9). It is good. But you can't think of "good" like you and I think of good. In the Hebrew this word for "good" (*tov*) means that the food was pleasant. And beautiful. And joyful. And precious. And delightful. That's what kind of food we are talking about in the garden.

Not only that, God explains to Adam and Eve that "every beast of the earth" and "every bird of the heavens" and "everything that creeps on the earth" and "everything that has the breath of life" has graciously been given "every green plant for food" to eat (Gen. 1:30).

That means everyone and everything has graciously been given what will sustain their life.

Let's think about this for a moment.

Adam and Eve, the beasts of the earth, the birds of the heavens, creeping things that creep on the earth, and everything that has breath of life is meant to eat from every green plant for food. Here is what's so amazing about grace. That just as God provided the necessary conditions for everything that has the breath of life to live, God also graciously provided the food that would sustain them. And it is good food (Gen. 2:9).

Thus, by God's grace, nothing was ever meant to boast in their self-sufficiency.

The first chapter of Genesis ends with "God saw everything that he had made, and behold, it was very good" (Gen. 1:31). This pronouncement is a little different than the conclusion of the previous days of creation.

Instead of saying that it was "good," now it was "very good."

This is but a mere window into how God demonstrated His grace before the Fall. Creation was not just a task to be performed, or an obligation to be met, but rather, creation was graciously designed to be enjoyed. His plan was for mankind to enjoy His grace.

For God, Adam and Eve were given dominion over the earth, which meant they would be keenly aware of how a hummingbird would fly, which is amazing enough, but He also wanted them to stop for a moment and enjoy the hummingbird in mid-flight. And if they had phones back then, I bet God would have loved for them to try and take a photo.

Or maybe they just blinked.

Rest

There are many days when I feel like quitting my job.

You might be thinking, *This just got awkward.*

But seriously, it happens, but why those thoughts enter my mind might be different than what you'd expect.

Here's why.

There is nothing better than teaching the Bible and theology every day. That is, until you experience getting in front of people who have no idea that Lolly has just kindly revealed some sin in my life. Then my dream job slowly becomes a nightmare that I can't escape.

Getting in front of people and teaching them about a holy (not me), good (not me), sinless (not me), gracious (not me), and merciful (not me) God is at best humbling. At worst, I'm left to feel like a fake and a fraud.

See, you would want to quit your job too.

In those moments, there is profound unrest within my soul as I stand there and think, *Surely, someone else should be doing this.*

On the other hand, when Lolly and I talk it through, and listen to each other, and forgive each other and move on, we have a new and strengthened sense of security knowing that we are no longer divided. That sense of unity puts my mind and heart at rest.

It's indescribable what the feeling of rest can do for the soul. When one human is at rest with another. It's almost like this is the way things were meant to be.

Our relationship with God is no different.

We recognize unrest there too. We know when we have sinned. We know when we have done something wrong. And then we wonder if God will forgive us. We wonder if God still loves us.

This is unrest.

Yet there is something so spiritually refreshing when we confess our sin to God—when we confess our unrest.

And what's on the other side of that confession is a promise only to be fulfilled by God. It's a promise of forgiveness and of a restored relationship. A promise of rest. But this kind of rest is only given by God's grace, as we are cleansed by the precious blood of Jesus (1 John 1:7).

This is where spiritual rest comes from. It comes from the reality that God loves you. That He has offered Himself as a sacrifice for you. That you are forgiven.

In that moment our spirit takes in a deep sigh of relief as we are restored back into the light of fellowship with God.

It's as though this is how God created things to be.

At rest.

At rest with God. At rest with one another.

Our spirits long for rest.

But do you know where this longing for rest comes from?

Let's go back to Genesis.

Creation is now finished.

Notice the finality to the language used in Genesis 2:1–3: "Thus the heavens and the earth were *finished*, and all the host of them. And on the seventh day God *finished* his work that he *had done*, and he rested on the seventh day from all his work that he *had done*. So God blessed the seventh day and made it holy, because on it God rested from all his work that he *had done* in creation."

With creation now complete, what does God do? The Bible says, "And he rested on the seventh day."

In His creation, God lavished on humans an abundance of grace by creating everything. This becomes the foundation for how we have fellowship with God. Without creation it wouldn't be possible to know God. Without creation there wouldn't be anything, nor anyone, to know God.

Then on the seventh day God rests. But notice that God doesn't rest alone, God doesn't retire to His own solitary place. Rather God graciously provides a precise location called the garden of Eden. And it is here where we find God at rest *with* Adam and Eve *within* the very world He has created (Gen. 2:1–3). This is the way things were meant to be.

Theologically, this is what it means to be at rest.

One thing worth pointing out is that the first six days of creation from Genesis 1 followed a certain pattern:

"And there was evening and there was morning, the first day" (v. 5).

"And there was evening and there was morning, the second day" (v. 8).

"And there was evening and there was morning, the third day" (v. 13).

"And there was evening and there was morning, the fourth day" (v. 19).

"And there was evening and there was morning, the fifth day" (v. 23).

"And there was evening and there was morning, the sixth day" (v. 31).

The seventh day is different though.

On the seventh day there is no pronouncement that "there was evening and there was morning, the seventh day."

It's almost like the seventh day never ended.

What are we supposed to do with that?

What if it means that even today, the seventh day has never concluded.

What are we supposed to do with *that*?

What if the lack of conclusion to the seventh day means that God's story is continuing to unfold? Even to this moment. What if that also means that grace is continuing to unfold? What if, from the start, all that Jesus has created is invited to dwell with God? And not just for the day, but forever? What if how God originally created things to be was good? In fact, very good.

If this was how things were supposed to be, then wouldn't it make sense that creation longs to rest? That humans created in God's image long to rest.

What Adam and Eve and the rest of creation is unaware of is that the Fall is about to occur. And this is going to change how we rest in God's presence. We'll talk a lot about this in Part Two.

At this point though, we could ask a few questions; for example, if God is resting, then who is in control of the world? If Jesus rests on the seventh day, then what do we do with His work on the cross when He died for our sins? If Jesus is not only the Creator, but also the one who upholds the universe. Doesn't sustaining and upholding the world take work and not rest?

There is a difference between the completed work of creation and God's work within what He has already created.

There is some tension here.

And just so you know, my goal won't be to alleviate the tension. I'm not sure that is even possible when trying to understand God. My hope is to provide a way for us to rest in the tension.

Here is the tension. There is a difference between the completed work of creation and God's work within what He has already created. God accomplished all He intended to create in those six days, and then on the seventh day He rested. But that doesn't mean God is unable to meticulously work within what He has created as He brings about His sovereign plan for creation. In other words, the "rest" in Genesis 2:1–3 is in reference to the completion of the first six days of creation, not to how God would uphold creation throughout the course of human history after those six days.

To illustrate this, let's use an example we have already talked about. Remember from the gospel of Matthew and that time when Jesus was resting in the boat in the middle of the storm (Matt. 8:24)? Remember how the disciples were freaking out and they woke Jesus up from His rest so that He might do something about it (v. 26)? Remember what Jesus did? He calmed the storm. He brought rest to the created order. In addition, He brought rest to His disciples as they no longer thought they were going to die. But according to Genesis 2:1–3, isn't God resting? So how can Jesus be doing the work of calming the storm?

This is the tension.

And here is how we might rest in that tension.

The work of creation is complete. Jesus was not calming a storm unfamiliar to the world that He has created. That is why He is never fearful or surprised by the storm. However, the world is still in need of Jesus to uphold what He has created. Which is why the storm listens to its Creator and calms down.

I don't want to ruin the ending, but let's just say there is a lot more to come as it relates to the seventh day of rest. I can't wait to show you. But we have so much more to see before we get there. However, at this point in the story, know that grace was intended to provide rest for creation. And rest is inseparably linked to being in God's presence. To having a relationship with Him.

This was enough.

This will always be enough.

CHAPTER 6

Equality

To this point in the story of God's grace we have made our way through the entire creation account. All seven days. We looked at the various ways God has lavished and designed grace so that we might dwell with Him. However, we need to go back to the sixth day just for a moment.

Because what we are going to find is that God's gracious plan for Adam and Eve was that they would be equal.

Not identical, so that they are one and the same.

But equal.

Not hierarchical, so that one might rule over the other, but with gracious equality.

This is the way it was supposed to be.

And the reason why has everything to do with who God is.

One of the first things we explored is that Jesus is the Creator. But this work of Jesus wasn't because the other members of the Trinity were absent at creation; rather it was always a Trinitarian decision that creation would be *by*, *through*, and *for* Christ.

For example, Paul wrote of Jesus, "He is the image of the invisible God, the firstborn of all creation. For *by* him all things were created, in heaven and on earth, visible and invisible, whether thrones or dominions or rulers or authorities—all things were created *through* him and *for* him" (Col. 1:15–16).

But on the sixth day there is a change in the way creation is described. God proclaims, "Let *us* make man in *our* image, after *our* likeness" (Gen. 1:26).

So what is the big difference?

Thus far, we haven't had this kind of self-description of God throughout the creation account. For the first time the Trinity has revealed that something will be created in "our" image. Because of that, it is no longer only Jesus' unique role within creation. Instead, it's now all three persons of the Trinity. In other words, the "us" and "our" from Genesis 1:26 is in reference to the plurality found within the Trinity.

This is significant because God is doing something different. God is creating something in His Trinitarian image and likeness. God hasn't done that yet.

And what is this specific kind of creation?

It's man.

But what is "man" in reference to (Gen. 1:26)?

The Hebrew word for man (*adom*) can either mean man, mankind, or Adam.

How can you tell the difference?

Context.

Context is what will help us figure out how the word "man" is being used.

So which one is it?

I'm not sure "man" in Genesis 1:26 is only referring to Adam.

Here's why.

Because if that were the case, then the reference to the Trinity with "us" and "our" in Genesis 1:26 wouldn't be necessary.

Why?

Because Jesus could have simply created Adam after His likeness; for example, you would have Jesus (singular) creating Adam (singular). And if the Bible wanted to direct our attention to Jesus, and not to the Trinity, that would have been totally fine, because prior to day six in creation, Jesus was already responsible for creating.

But the Bible is very specific in Genesis 1:26 to describe that "man" was created in "our" image. Plural. Not singular. For that reason, I think "man" in Genesis 1:26 is actually mankind. Which makes more sense because there is plurality found within the personhood of mankind, just as there is plurality found in the personhood of the Trinity. And if man is to reflect the Trinity it would need to have plurality as part of its makeup. And we find that plurality within mankind.

Now you might be thinking, "Okay, this makes a little sense, but I'm not totally sure yet. How do we know that it is mankind and not Adam?"

The very next verse provides more clarity. It says, "So God created man in his own image, in the image of God he created him" (Gen. 1:27).

But that says the same thing as Genesis 1:26, which is still describing God's creation as "man."

I know, right?

But the next part of verse 27 is where it reveals what it means for God to create man in His image. The whole of verse 27 reads, "So God created man in his own image, in the image of God he created him; male and female he created them." What we find is that "man" in Genesis 1:26–27 is to include the creation of *both* the male and female.

> Not only are Adam and Eve created equally in the image of God, but they are to equally share in their dominion over everything that God has created.

Mankind.

This means Eve does not receive her image of God-ness from Adam, but that Eve received that from God when they were created equally in the image of God (Gen. 1:26–27).

There is another way God reveals the equality between Adam and Eve within creation. In Genesis 1:26 it says, "Let us make man in our image, after our likeness. And let them have dominion over the fish of the sea and over the birds of the heavens and over the livestock and over all the earth and over every creeping thing that creeps on the earth."

Who is supposed to have dominion over the fish and birds and livestock and the creeping things and the earth?

The Bible says, "And let *them*."

Who is them?

There is no indication from Genesis 1:26 who *them* is. All it references is that God creates man in His image. Then it says "And let them" have dominion.

Again, Genesis 1:27 helps clarify who it is that is supposed to have dominion over everything that God has previously created the last five days. And "them" is Adam and Eve. Genesis 1:27 says, "So God created man in his own image, in the image of God he created him; male and female he created *them*."

The same "them" from Genesis 1:26 to whom God gives dominion over everything is the same "them" in Genesis 1:27 that is used to describe the male and female being created in God's image.

This adds beautiful layers to the complexities found in the equality between Adam and Eve as image bearers of God. Not only are they created equally in the image of God, but they are to equally share in their dominion over everything that God has created.

Surely that doesn't mean that Adam and Eve are going to exercise their dominion in the same way. After all, they are different persons, with different talents, different gifts and abilities. But somehow, supernaturally, there is equality between them. And together this equality will contribute to how they are to exercise their dominion over the world.

Very soon everything is going to change.

After the Fall, one of the most significant differences is that there will no longer be perfect equality between Adam and Eve. Instead of sharing in their equal dominion over everything God has created, they will instead seek to have dominion over each other. But we can't move too quickly past this current reality within the story of God's grace. It isn't enough to simply acknowledge that there is equality because God created them, but we have to be even more specific. Adam and Eve reflect the very image of God. And God is triune.

This means no one member of the Trinity rules over the other. Rather, within the Trinity is a beautiful, mutual indwelling of the Father, the Son, and Holy Spirit. Meaning, they live in perfect community with one another. It is from this gracious relationship shared within the Trinity that we see God's intention in how He created mankind.

By God's grace, this was the way things were meant to be.

CHAPTER 7

Helper

Have you ever wondered what God was doing prior to creation? Do you think God ever got bored or lonely?

I actually think prior to creation God was perfectly content.

You might be thinking, "How do you know?"

I don't know.

But based on who God is, it would make good sense that He wouldn't get lonely because with God there has always been perfect communion shared between the Father, Son, and Holy Spirit.

Moreover, God didn't need to create the world in order to justify or validate anything within Himself. In fact, prior to creation God had nothing to prove and wasn't in need of anything relationally.

This is what makes creation so authentic and genuine, that God desired to bring forth creation, and particularly these creatures created in His image, so that He might have a relationship with them. This means that the very existence of humanity has a profound and eternal purpose from the start, which was to dwell with the one who created them. This is where our deepest desire for purpose finds its rest.

As amazing as this is, our relationship with God was never going to be enough.

Not enough?

Yes, not enough.

How can that be?

Genesis 2 helps us understand why, and once again it has everything to do with who God is.

In Genesis 2 we learn that Adam is created first, then Eve. It says,

> When no bush of the field was yet in the land and no small plant of the field had yet sprung up—for the LORD God had not caused it to rain on the land, and there was no man to work the ground, and a mist was going up from the land and was watering the whole face of the ground—then the LORD God formed the man of dust from the ground and breathed into his nostrils the breath of life, and the man became a living creature. (Gen. 2:5–7)

Hold on, did you notice that right in the middle of this passage it says, "There was no man to work the ground"? Then it also describes how God formed the man with the dust from the ground.

The last time we discussed the meaning of "man" it was in reference to mankind, which included both Adam and Eve (Gen. 1:26–27). So is "man" in the verses above also talking about mankind?

Remember that we talked about how the Hebrew word for man (*adom*) could mean either man, mankind, or Adam? And remember how we talked about the only way to tell the difference is based on the context of the passage?

That applies here too.

And the context seems to indicate that Genesis 2:5–7 is talking about Adam and not mankind.

Here's why. In Genesis 2 we don't learn of Eve's creation until much later in the chapter (Gen. 2:18–23). In addition, Adam is described as being alone in the garden to "work it and keep it," which seems to indicate that Eve wasn't created yet (Gen. 2:15).

It's somewhat confusing, right?

In Genesis 1 both Adam and Eve are equally created on the sixth day. But in Genesis 2 Adam is created first, then Eve.

In light of this, how are we supposed to read Genesis 1–2?

We have to withhold the urge to read Genesis 2 as *the* story about how Adam and Eve were created.

In other words, let Genesis 1 be about the creation of everything—which includes the sixth day when mankind is created in the image of God (Gen. 1:26–27).

That means, by the time we get to Genesis 2:1–3 creation is finished. This is important as we get further into Genesis 2, because what we end up discovering is more about the creation event. And what we find out is more about *how* Adam and Eve were created, even though they already existed.

However, the difficulty with reading Genesis 2 as *the* account as to how Adam and Eve were created has led some to conclude that since Adam was created first, and then Eve, that this demonstrates a kind of hierarchy within mankind. One in which man is to rule and have dominion over everything, including the woman. And to be fair, if one were to read Genesis 2 as *the* primary text for the creation of mankind, then that is a plausible conclusion.

But when you read Genesis 2 in light of what has already happened in Genesis 1, then there seems to be something else God is trying to reveal.

That Eve helps Adam fulfill what it means to be created in the image of God.

In Genesis 1:26–28 we discovered that mankind (male and female), is equally created in the image of God. They have different roles, but equal in their dominion over creation. But why does God make us aware of that story first? Why does God first emphasize that Adam and Eve are equal (Gen. 1), and then unravel how Adam is created first (Gen. 2)?

My guess is that there is a larger story going on.

And if it is God's story, it must be a gracious story.

It goes like this.

Adam will never be equal with God.

Why?

Because God is the Creator and Adam will always be the creature (Gen. 2:7).

Thus, with God as Adam's only companion, that means Adam will always be deficient relationally. That is why God said, "It is not good that man should be alone" (Gen. 2:18).

Think about it. Adam is technically not alone; he is with God in the garden of Eden. Adam has God all to himself. Shouldn't that be the pinnacle of what it means to have a relationship? Yet, according to God, it is not good that Adam is alone.

> **Genesis is revealing how Adam and Eve together reflect who they are created in the image of: God is plural (three) yet one. Mankind is plural (two) yet one.**

But who was Adam created in the image of?

God.

And who is God?

God is one being, eternally existent as three persons (Father, Son, and Holy Spirit). As such, the three persons of the Trinity live equally together, and surely not alone.

Thus, Adam alone with no equal of his own doesn't make sense for this creature created in God's image because Adam lacks what it means to be created in God's image.

As a result, what does God do?

He creates a suitable helper for Adam—He creates Eve.

I have always wondered why in Genesis 1:26 it never mentions the numerical value of "us" and "our" in reference to God. It simply says, "Then God said, 'Let *us* make man in *our* image, after *our* likeness.'" It never describes God as Trinity; it simply leaves it with God being described in the plural.

What if this is because the whole purpose right then and there isn't to expound on the Trinity? What if instead Genesis is revealing how Adam and Eve together reflect who they are created in the image of?

God is plural (three) yet one.

Mankind is plural (two) yet one.

Which makes sense because mankind was created in the image of God.

Thus, Eve helps Adam fulfill what it means to be a human.

What if helper *doesn't* mean that women are less than men because Adam was created first? Helper *isn't* to say that women are to take care of the home while their husbands are at work . . . as though Adam could have done this on his own, but God decided that it would be better if Eve helped. Helper also doesn't mean a woman's only purpose is to take care of the kids.

By the way, being a stay-at-home mom is significant and hard and amazing and a gift to the family. Being at home with the kids has always been Lolly's dream. Honestly, it is more difficult than any "job" I've ever had. All I'm saying is I'm not convinced that's what "helper" means in Genesis.

Instead, helper is one of the most powerful theological words in the whole Bible.

It brings to light that it isn't good that Adam should be alone (Gen. 2:18).

Isn't good? you might be thinking.

But I thought that after God created Adam and Eve, He said that it was "very good" (Gen. 1:31)? So why in Genesis 2:18 does it describe Adam alone with God as "not good"? Remember earlier when we talked about how Genesis 2 is describing more about what happened in Genesis 1?

This is a good example of that.

In Genesis 1:26–27 the creation of both Adam and Eve is complete and thus it is very good. However, when God describes Adam as "not good" in Genesis 2:18, it is a statement concerning Adam as an image bearer of God prior to Eve. In other words, Genesis 2:18 gives us a snapshot of what took place in Genesis 1:26–27 before it was "very good." Which means there was a moment during the sixth day when it wasn't good.

Eve helps Adam fulfill what is required to reflect God's image.

Have you ever wondered why Eve was taken from Adam's side and not from the ground like everything else that was created?

Eve came from Adam because she was to be equal with him. Thus, Adam says, "This at last is bone of my bones and flesh of my flesh; she shall be called Woman, because she was taken out of Man" (Gen. 2:23). With Eve, mankind receives a gracious gift, and mankind finally is able to reflect who they were created in the image of.

Well, almost.

The second to last verse in Genesis 2 says, "Therefore a man shall leave his father and his mother and hold fast to his wife, and they shall become one flesh" (v. 24). If you have ever been to a wedding, I'm sure the pastor recited this verse at some point.

For most Christians the idea that two flesh become one flesh means that the husband and wife have sex. However, there is more to this one-flesh thing than physical intimacy.

This verse completes the image of "helper" from Genesis 2:18.

What is our definition of the Trinity again? That God is one being, eternally existent as three persons. And who is mankind created in the image of? The triune God. That means that mankind must have plurality and singularity.

Together, Genesis 1–2 reveals both to us.

We see the plurality in that it wasn't good for Adam to be alone, so God created Eve to provide an equal for Adam to live in community with. And not just any community, but the most intimate form of relationship. This relationship is to reflect the equality found within the Trinity.

Then, at the very end of Genesis 2 we see the pronouncement that Adam and Eve are not just two flesh, but rather one flesh. At the same time. This demonstrates the singularity (or oneness) within mankind, which completes who Adam and Eve were created in the image of.

In other words, God reveals Himself to us, through us.

Without Eve's help, mankind would never reflect God's gracious image.

CHAPTER 8

Forever

Who would have thought that there would be this much grace to be explored in the first few chapters of the Bible?

Yet there is still one more observation we need to make before everything changes.

In just the last chapter we looked at marriage as one of the ways God has graciously revealed Himself to us. That in marriage when two believers commit themselves to one another before God, something happens. These two distinct people become one.

One flesh.

An important verse that reveals this supernatural reality is Genesis 2:24, which says, "Therefore a man shall leave his father and his mother and hold fast to his wife, and they shall become one flesh." As a result, when God graciously joins something together it is never meant to be separated.

Think about it.

Name one time in the Bible when God joined something together only to separate it.

It goes against who God is and what He has created.

As a result, marriage is far more than a civil union.

More than a commitment to each other.

It is sacred and holy.

And for Christians, marriage reflects who God is.

Take the Trinity for example.

The persons of the Trinity (the Father, Son, and Holy Spirit) will never be separated from one another. God is one being, eternally existent as three persons. Never to be confused or mixed *or separated*. And yet they are eternally one. There will never be a time when this isn't the case.

Another example is the hypostatic union.

Hypostatic what?

The hypostatic union is the belief that Jesus, in the incarnation, adds to Himself full humanity without forgoing or limiting *or separating* His deity. Thus, Christians affirm that Jesus, the second person of the Trinity, has a fully divine nature and a fully human nature.

This dual nature of Christ will never be separated. Jesus will forever have a physical body after the incarnation.

How about the resurrection?

What happens to your body when you die? It is buried in the ground.

But what happens to your spirit? Does it die too?

No.

The Bible promises that for Christians, when we die our spirits go to be with the Lord immediately (2 Cor. 5:8).

Shoot!

This might not be a helpful example, because if my body is buried in the ground and my spirit is with the Lord, then what the Lord has joined together is separated.

However, who does the separating at death?

It's not God.

Sin separates us.

Death is the result of the Fall.

But watch this—when Jesus returns and the dead are raised, what happens?

Our bodies, now glorified, are reunited with our spirits. We are given glorified bodies designed to last forever.

We are going to talk a lot about this in Part Three.

Do you see the trend here? What God has graciously joined together is to remain one forever.

Let's look at one more example.

Speaking of marriage. You know what is a great topic to bring up next time you are spending time with a bunch of Christians?

Submission.

Christians love this topic.

I mean, who doesn't like to talk about what it looks like for a wife to submit to your husband. Lolly and I talk about this all the time.

I'm kidding. We don't actually.

There is a rather famous passage in Ephesians 5 written by the apostle Paul. Who was single by the way.

He begins by talking about how wives should submit to their husbands (v. 22). He even says that the husband is the head of the wife and Paul uses the church as his example (v. 23). Paul writes, "For the husband is the head of the wife even as Christ is the head of the church, his body, and is himself its Savior. Now as the church submits to Christ, so also wives should submit in everything to their husbands" (Eph. 5:23–24).

Then Paul turns his attention to the husbands. He calls the husbands to love their wives, but it is a specific kind of love. Husbands are to love their wives as "Christ loved the church and gave himself up for her, that he might sanctify her, having cleansed her by the washing of water with the word, so that he might present the church to himself in splendor, without spot or wrinkle or any such thing, that she might be holy and without blemish" (vv. 25–27).

But notice what Paul does next.

He quotes the Old Testament, saying, "For no one ever hated his own flesh, but nourishes and cherishes it, just as Christ does the church, because we are members of his body. 'Therefore a man shall leave his father and mother and hold fast to his wife, and the two shall become one flesh'" (vv. 29–31).

Wait a second! Paul quotes Genesis 2:24.

Then he says, "This mystery is profound, and I am saying that it refers to Christ and the church" (v. 32).

Regardless of your views of submission, what Paul is ultimately drawing our attention to is the relationship the church shares with Christ. He likens the church to a bride, whose groom is Christ. The church is always to submit to her husband.

And by appealing to Genesis 2:24, Paul is saying the church and Christ are one flesh. In other words, the church and Christ are never meant to be separated. Never does the Bible indicate that there is a time in which Christ is cut off or separated from His church.

Of all the examples, marriage is the strongest imagery Paul can think of to illustrate the oneness shared between Christ and the church. And Genesis 2:24 becomes the foundation for his argument.

This is beautiful.

When God graciously announces that Adam and Eve have become one flesh, what has become one is never meant to be two flesh again. Even though they would always remain male and female, their one-fleshness wasn't supposed to change. Ever.

What Paul isn't doing is elevating marriage as something to be obsessed over. Paul wasn't married. Jesus wasn't married. At times, Paul even talks about how it would be beneficial not to get married (e.g., 1 Cor. 7:6–7). However, Paul still understands there is a deep and gracious mystery in marriage, that two flesh becoming one flesh is the most powerful unifying moment between two creatures created in God's image.

Why is this gracious oneness so important?

Because the Fall is about to happen.

And as a result, all kinds of consequences befall Adam and Eve. One of those realities is death and separation from one another. But just because death and separation are part of our natural world after the Fall doesn't mean that was the way it was supposed to be. God didn't design grace to separate us. The declaration that "a man shall leave his father and mother and hold fast to his wife, and the two shall become one flesh," was intended to last forever.

Grace makes forever possible.

CHAPTER 9

Be Like God

Early on in my faith I remember hearing a lot about Adam and Eve and having a very negative feeling toward them. It was as though they were to blame for everything bad that has ever happened.

However, through the lens of grace my perspective has changed. I see things differently. What I see now is a dramatic story inherently linked to a relationship Adam and Eve desired to have with God.

Remember in Genesis 2:18, when Adam was in the very presence of God, and yet there was a time when it wasn't good?

Remember why?

Because while being in the very presence of God, there was still something within Adam that was lonely. The Bible even described how Adam was in need of help (Gen. 2:18). Which makes sense because as a creature created in the image of the triune God, equality in companionship is essential as the Father, Son, and Holy Spirit share in perfect communion with one another. Thus, God graciously provided Adam and Eve with each other and together they were to enjoy their relationship with God.

However, God commanded Adam not to eat the fruit of this one particular tree in the middle of the garden. He said, "You may surely eat of every tree of the garden, but of the tree of the knowledge of good and evil you shall not eat, for in the day that you eat of it you shall surely die" (Gen.

71

2:16–17). God didn't forbid them from doing a lot of things because, as we discussed earlier, God wanted them to enjoy His creation. However, there was this one thing He asked Adam not to do.

But why not eat from that tree?

The Bible tells us that *every tree* in the garden was beautiful and produced delicious food to eat. And this would have included the tree of life and the tree of the knowledge of good and evil (Gen. 2:9).

To be honest, God never tells us why.

We are just told that God commanded them not to eat of that one particular tree.

God's word should have been a good enough reason.

In Genesis 3 we are introduced to another character, the serpent.

I don't like snakes.

At all.

They gross me out and make my knees feel weak.

Have I told you about my father-in-law? His name is Ted. And Ted is a cowboy. Like a real one.

I'll have to tell you sometime about how he wouldn't let me marry Lolly until I pulled back his seventy-pound compound bow. And let's just say I failed the first time. And by failed, I mean my shoulder dislocated. But like any great story I fought back and married the girl!

Where Lolly's parents live there are a lot of rattlesnakes.

Some of them are big. Insert weak knees.

Sometimes they get too close to the house or animals, and unfortunately, Ted has to kill the snake.

But if he does that, he keeps them in order to skin them.

Ted makes all kinds of beautiful things from the skin. And rattlesnakes have a beautiful coloring. Here is my favorite part though. When you go over to the house and you open the freezer, you have to brace yourself, because that's where Ted keeps all the snakes. So you will likely find three or four frozen headless rattlesnakes in there at any given time.

Who's coming over for Thanksgiving?

Back to the serpent.

The Bible describes how the serpent "was more crafty than any other beast of the field" (Gen. 3:1). And by crafty, Satan is using God's words to deceive. The serpent says, "Did God actually say, 'You shall not eat of any tree in the garden'?" (Gen. 3:1).

Eve's response to the serpent was, "We may eat of the fruit of the trees in the garden, but God said, 'You shall not eat of the fruit of the tree that is in the midst of the garden, neither shall you touch it, lest you die'" (vv. 2–3).

But then the serpent retorts, "You will not surely die. For God knows that when you eat of it your eyes will be opened, and you will be like God, knowing good and evil" (vv. 4–5).

You know, the serpent isn't totally wrong. In order to deceive someone, you can't be totally wrong. With deception, there has to be some truth. And Satan is a master at disguising himself as truth.

God said that if they eat from the tree of the knowledge of good and evil they will die. But Satan is right because after Adam and Eve ate from the tree of the knowledge of good and evil they don't die.

In fact, they keep living.

The Bible even describes how Adam and Eve clothed themselves and hid from God's presence (v. 7).

After the Fall, life becomes restless.

Dwelling with God feels unnatural.

It's as though sin has an adverse reaction to being in God's presence.

That's why the serpent's response to Eve wasn't a complete lie. Adam and Eve don't immediately fall to the ground and die. Instead, what Satan does is disguise himself as truth when he isn't. He portrays himself as an angel of light, when in fact, he is just a crafty serpent.

Take something as serious as murder, for example. Satan knows you might be alarmed if he were to tell you to murder someone. Thus, Satan lures your heart into anger toward your brother or sister. That is much more acceptable to us. But remember Jesus' words, that whether you murder someone or are angry with your brother, you are "liable to judgment" (Matt. 5:21–26).

This is what Satan does.

According to the serpent in Genesis 3, Adam and Eve wouldn't die if they eat the fruit. But here is how Satan is deceiving them. It's their spiritual death. Adam and Eve immediately die spiritually upon eating the fruit from the tree of the knowledge of good and evil.

They miss this.

Then what does the serpent say?

He tells Eve that if they eat of the fruit, they will become "like God" (Gen. 3:5).

According to the serpent the result of eating from this one particular tree is that Adam and Eve will be like God. This is where my negative opinions about Adam and Eve came from.

The Bible is all about God's desire to have a relationship with us.

But is that fair?

I'm not sure.

I'm beginning to have a more gracious opinion toward Adam and Eve. Here's what I mean. Creatures aren't supposed to be like their Creator. That is why God graciously gave Adam and Eve to each other so that they would have each other as equals, because God knew they could never be equal with Him.

The Bible is all about God's desire to have a relationship with us. God creates everything and then rests with and within His creation.

I don't think Adam and Eve were conspiring to overthrow heaven and sit on God's throne. Besides, God has already given them power and dominion over everything.

What more power do you need?

That might've been Satan's desire, but I'm not convinced that is what Adam and Eve were after. I think they wanted to relate to God as equals. They wanted to share in the relationship they witnessed between the Father, Son, and Holy Spirit.

Adam and Eve probably looked at themselves as image bearers of God and thought, we have some of God's attributes, we are different people and yet we are one flesh, just like God. We can love one another, just like God. We can create things, just like God. So why can't we be like Him and eat from this tree?

Yet that wasn't how things were supposed to be.

Instead, they were to be content as creatures.

And Satan capitalized on Adam's and Eve's desire, and they ate from the tree of the knowledge of good and evil. The Bible says, "So when the woman saw that the tree was good for food, and that it was a delight to the eyes, and that the tree was to be desired to make one wise, she took of its fruit and ate, and she also gave some to her husband who was with her, and he ate" (Gen. 3:6).

Just like that, everything changes. Dwelling with God will be different. God doesn't change, but how we rest in God's presence will.

The Bible says, "Then the eyes of both were opened, and they knew that they were naked. And they sewed fig leaves together and made themselves loincloths" (v. 7).

Things are now not the way they were supposed to be. The relationship between Adam and Eve would need a lot of help in order to make it work. The creation which Adam and Eve were given dominion over would be difficult to care for.

Have you ever wondered what will happen in the new heaven and the new earth if someone messes up and sins again? Have you ever wondered if we will have to start all over again with a new redemptive plan?

Oh boy.

We have to wait until Part Three for those answers.

PART TWO

Grace
After the
Fall

Introduction to Part Two

Thus far, we have spent the majority of our time in the first two chapters of Genesis, right where we needed to be. It was in those chapters that we discovered how God's relationship with mankind was meant to be.

However, everything is about to change. Humanity's story is going to take a dreadful turn. But what makes it so grim is that for the first time mankind will find itself longing to dwell in God's presence. To this point, no one had felt that unrest.

But make no mistake: Even though everything changes, God doesn't.

He can't.

It's part of who God is that He would never change.

Which means Adam and Eve are experiencing the same grace prior to the Fall that will make it possible to dwell in God's presence after the Fall.

Humanity doesn't know what grace is capable of yet. But they will soon find out.

This is what's so amazing about God's grace. Even though sin is going to affect everything, what sin doesn't change is God's desire and plan to dwell with us.

But it won't be easy.

In fact, it will seem unfair at times. It will be complicated. Even mysterious. Yet it will also be beautiful. And necessary. Full of hope. And even help explain our deepest longings.

In Part Two we will look at the Fall, the prophet Jonah, the Prodigal Son, and the passion of Christ as our examples of how God's grace meets us right where we are.

From the beginning, mankind was created to dwell with God, which was only made possible through the work of Jesus in creation. Nothing changes after the Fall. Dwelling with God will continue to be possible only by the grace of the Lord Jesus.

CHAPTER 10

Things Are Different

What might seem like just another verse in the Bible is no ordinary verse at all. It actually represents a change within the course of human history.

Who knew so much could happen with just one verse?

In Genesis 3:6, the scene is described like this: "So when the woman saw that the tree was good for food, and that it was a delight to the eyes, and that the tree was to be desired to make one wise, she took of its fruit and ate, and she also gave some to her husband who was with her, and he ate."

And just like that, sin enters the human story.

And in the aftermath, God's relationship with everything He has created will now be different.

As Christians we call this moment the Fall.

One might ask, "But what kind of changes are we talking about?"

Remember earlier when we discussed how Adam and Eve were created *equal* and that *together* they were to rule over God's creation (Gen. 1:26–27)?

Now the Bible describes that Eve will undergo pain in childbearing. Not only that, but Eve's desires "shall be contrary" to her husband, and he will even "rule over" her (Gen. 3:16).

Things are different.

Also remember when "the LORD God took the man and put him in the garden of Eden to work it and keep it" (Gen. 2:15)? Then God told Adam, "You may surely eat of every tree of the garden, but of the tree of the knowledge of good and evil you shall not eat" (vv. 16–17). Ironically, the Fall happens in the same garden that Adam was to care for, protect, and work in.

Now, as a result of the Fall, God tells Adam, "In pain you shall eat of it all the days of your life; thorns and thistles it shall bring forth for you; and you shall eat the plants of the field" (Gen. 3:17–18).

From the beginning, Adam was meant to enjoy his work. He was created to exercise great care over God's creation. However, what was originally meant to be enjoyed, he will now find painful and empty.

Change is a difficult concept. Humans don't like change. So much so that we sometimes describe humanity as "creatures of habit."

Every academic year one of the busiest seasons is right before we break for the holidays. Grades are due. Classes are concluding. Final exams are being held. And yet, I've come to terms with the reality that not a lot of grading will get done. But the reason for this lack of productivity is because some of my students are wanting to meet and talk and pray.

Each student has a little different story, but the struggle is the same.

They are not looking forward to going home.

For many, home is not restful because they don't feel emotionally safe or comfortable.

As a result, they become anxious, and they don't know what to do.

We all have those relationships where we desperately want to love someone; however, we aren't entirely sure what version of them we will get.

What is unfortunate is that we are tempted to take this emotional experience with an unpredictable person and begin to think God is this way. That God is not safe. And that with God you never can be sure what you'll get.

But is that fair?

Even though we are created in God's image, that doesn't mean God is the embodiment of our human flaws.

This is how powerful it is for humans to be created in God's image. When people experience Christians, they are in a way experiencing what God is like. Which is terrifying when we don't embody Jesus with our lives. We are doing far more damage than simply not living a good Christian life. We are shaping how people perceive who God is.

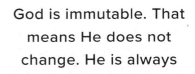

God is immutable. That means He does not change. He is always love. Always merciful. Always just.

In theology we use "immutability" to describe God. It means God does not change. It's within His very character to remain the same. That means that God is always love. Always merciful. Always just. Always gracious. No matter the human circumstances.

A verse in the Bible that describes God's immutability is James 1:17, which says, "Every good and every perfect gift is from above, coming down from the Father of lights, with whom there is no variation or shadow due to change." The idea that God does not change is confusing and unrelatable because we change all the time. Our personalities change, our opinions change, our desires change.

Change is just a part of life.

In some cases, we change for the better as we become more like Jesus. However, in other ways, due to sin, we may change for the worse.

But what might the immutability of God have to do with grace?

In order to know what grace is capable of, we must first understand that if God does not change, this also means that grace will never change.

Why?

Because God is gracious.

What makes this thought so beautiful and comforting is that, even though we are constantly changing, God never does. While we are in process, God is steady and gentle, so as to never leave us nor forsake us.

With Adam and Eve we are reminded that God always remains faithful to us, even in our most faithless moments.

CHAPTER 11

A New Kind of Grace?

Let's just say having three young boys at home is never boring. Not too long ago I started to notice all these new plants around the house. I asked Lolly what was going on and she said, "Those are my girls."

But she said it with a facial expression like, *What about this don't you get?*

I get that face a lot.

I looked at her somewhat confused, thinking, "There is a lot about this I don't get."

In our marriage we have these conversations all the time. With just our facial expressions. Then Lolly said, pointing to each plant and waving, "Hi, Lola. Hi, Stephanie. Hi, Jashlene."

Still confused and a little worried about my wife, she said, "I need some more girls around here."

I said, "So you bought plants?"

She said, "Well, it was that or another dog."

To which I quickly replied, "Hi, Lola. Hi, Stephanie. Hi, Jashlene."

Children are truly a gift from God, and Lolly and I have never taken any of her pregnancies for granted. Thinking back though, something has happened each time we've found out Lolly is pregnant. At some point we wondered if we could love this new baby as much as we love the others.

But then you go to the doctor for the first time and everything changes.

You hear the thumping little heartbeat for the first time and everything changes.

You see the first ultrasound images and everything changes.

Then the baby is born, and your heart explodes all over again.

It's unexplainable, but your capacity to love expands right before your eyes. It's like there was room within your heart you didn't know existed. Yet no pregnancy surprises God, which means that even though Lolly and I were wondering if there was room in our hearts, God knew all along that this love was within us.

In other words, each child doesn't possess a different kind of love from Lolly and me.

Grace truly is magnificent and powerful.

Instead, we've come to discover that the same love within us grows and expands without ever changing.

Grace is a lot like a parent's love for their child.

Prior to the Fall (Gen. 1:1–3:5), it was God's grace that provided Adam and Eve with all they would need to have a relationship with God. They were to dwell with God and enjoy one another and His creation.

After the Fall (Gen. 3:6–Rev. 20), Adam and Eve had a relationship with God; however, it would now be different as a result of sin. But in order to have a relationship with Adam and Eve, God did not change. He can't because God is immutable.

So Adam and Eve were experiencing the same grace after the Fall that was sustaining their relationship with God prior to the Fall. In other words, Adam and Eve were simply learning something new about grace that had always already existed.

Here is what is even crazier. You and I are living in a period of human history still affected by the Fall and sin nature. We are still waiting for Jesus to return and to make all things new. Yet we still have a relationship with God, and it is only by His grace that we are able to dwell with Him.

But here is the thing: We are experiencing today the same grace that Adam and Eve did prior to the Fall. In other words, we are also experiencing right now the same grace that will sustain and uphold our relationship with God after the Fall in the new heaven and the new earth (Rev. 21–22). We just don't know what that feels like yet.

Thus, it wasn't just because sin entered the world that suddenly there was this need for grace in order to have a relationship with God.

It's always been grace.

And it will always be grace.

Because God loves us, He has chosen to graciously meet us right where we are.

Grace truly is magnificent and powerful.

Have you ever noticed what God's reaction to Adam and Eve was like after the Fall? It describes God as walking in the garden.

Not panicked.

But walking.

As the Bible describes the scene, "They heard the sound of the Lord God walking in the garden in the cool of the day" (Gen. 3:8).

And God calmly calls out for Adam and Eve. "Where are you?" as though He doesn't know where they are or what they've done (v. 9).

But he knows. He's God.

This monumental moment that changes everything does not catch God off guard as though He doesn't know what to do. Or that He doesn't have a plan.

No.

He's prepared.

In fact, He's been graciously prepared for this moment since before the foundation of the world.

CHAPTER 12

Where Are You?

Remember how God was walking in the garden, not running around in a panic, in the cool of the day? Let's go back to that moment (Gen. 3:8–13), but this time looking closely at Adam's and Eve's reaction toward God.

The Bible describes how the "eyes" of Adam and Eve were "opened," and they knew they were naked (Gen. 3:7). Fully aware and vulnerable, they become insecure with each other and sew fig leaves together to clothe themselves. In other words, their new natural impulse was to hide from each other.

Then the Bible describes Adam's and Eve's reaction to God's presence. Right after the Fall we learn "the man and his wife *hid themselves* from the *presence* of the LORD God" (v. 8).

This is what sin does.

Sin creates within us a desire to no longer rest in God's presence.

Sin brings into the world a kind of unrest deep within us that has a negative spiritual reaction to being in God's presence.

But this shouldn't surprise us.

Why?

What do you and I do when we sin?

We hide from God's presence.

We might not literally clothe ourselves with fig leaves. But we might resist confessing that sin to God.

Perhaps we are fearful that God won't forgive us. Or instead of confessing our sin we might make a personal decision that we will never do *that* sin again and just give it some time for the guilt to wear off.

But 1 John 1:8 says this about hiding sin from God—"If we say we have no sin, we deceive ourselves, and the truth is not in us." The only person we are fooling is ourselves by attempting to hide our sin from God.

Moreover, 1 John 1:10 says, "If we say we have not sinned, we make him a liar, and his word is not in us."

Make Him a liar about what?

About sin in our lives.

God's Word says that "all have sinned and fall short of the glory of God" (Rom. 3:23).

We were not created to hide. By grace, we were created to live in the light of community with one another and with God.

You can't make that claim while hiding your sin from God.

But unfortunately, we still try.

What about others? Maybe if we've sinned against someone else, we attempt to "hide" by avoiding that person for a while. Maybe we hope everyone will just get over it and move on.

Isn't this what makes relationships so hard?

When I sin against Lolly, I can't hide from her. I've tried before. It doesn't work.

Why?

We live in the same house. We eat at the same table. We get ready in the same bathroom. We sleep in the same bed. That's why in marriage two flesh becoming one flesh is so much more spiritually complex than physical intimacy.

But isn't it beautiful that the way in which humans reconcile with God or one another is by no longer hiding? This takes humility and a firm dependency on the grace of God to confront the reality of sin in our lives.

In other words, we were not created to hide.

By grace, we were created to live in the light of community with one another and with God.

If you think about it, it's quite amazing that Eve helps Adam reflect in whose image they are made. No one person of the Trinity is trying to hide from the other. It isn't like the Holy Spirit has ever sinned against the Son and, as a result, is trying to hide from Jesus. That is unimaginable. It's anti-Trinitarian. That said, even though sin makes it feel natural for us to want to hide and even run away, that isn't the way it was supposed to be.

The reality whereby we attempt to hide from God, or someone else, is as old as Genesis 3:6. That means even though we don't sew fig leaves together and clothe ourselves like Adam and Eve when we sin, we still have our own ways of hiding from God's presence.

But let's not miss this either. God permitted Adam and Eve to hide from His presence. Nothing happens outside of God's sovereignty. Thus, the permission to hide from His presence is only made possible by God's grace. So that even today when we attempt to hide from God's presence, we are doing so by God's permission. By His grace.

Why would God do this?

Because He has a plan to meet us right where we are. In our naked, raggedly clothed, hidden places.

And by His grace, God also provides humans with the ability to return to Him and dwell in His presence once again.

You want to know how? I'll show you really soon.

CHAPTER 13

Clothed

Do you remember the first instance of grace in the Bible? It was found in the very first verse: "In the beginning, God created the heavens and the earth" (Gen. 1:1).

And even though the word grace doesn't appear, we concluded that the word "created" had gracious meaning within it. That God brought forth something and gave it to mankind as a gracious gift.

A gift to be enjoyed with God forever.

Forever?

Yes.

Remember how on the final day of creation God rests?

And remember how that day never ended?

It just keeps going.

Thus, we were created to rest with God forever.

Then everything changed.

Remember why it changed?

Adam and Eve ate the fruit and sinned. As a result, everything would be different. But what's so incredible is that even though everything changed as a result of sin, God never changed. He can't, which also means that grace didn't change either.

The same grace that provided the necessary conditions for Adam and

Eve to have a relationship with God prior to the Fall is the same grace that provides the necessary conditions for them to have a relationship with God after the Fall.

God knew (and knows) everything. From the beginning God planned for grace to work this way.

If the first instance of grace is found with the word "created" from Genesis 1:1, then where is the first instance of grace found in the Bible after the Fall?

It didn't take God but fifteen verses to introduce us to grace after the Fall. "And the LORD God made for Adam and for his wife garments of skins and clothed them."

You might be thinking, "So where is the grace?"

> If you understand the effectiveness of God's grace to be that He fixes your problems, then you will likely live in a state of continual letdown with Him.

Just as with the word "created" in Genesis 1:1, this time grace is found hidden within the word "clothed."

Let me explain.

After the Fall Adam and Eve clothe themselves with fig leaves because they realized that they're naked.

That must have been awkward.

Then Adam and Eve hear God walking toward them and for the first time they hide from Him (Gen. 3:8).

But God calls out for them. "Where are you?"

To which Adam responds, "I heard the sound of you in the garden, and I was afraid, because I was naked, and I hid myself" (v. 10). We see that one of the first known effects of sin on humanity is a desire to avoid dwelling with God.

Then the Lord turns immediately to rebuke the serpent (vv. 14–15). Then the Lord admonishes Eve (v. 16). Finally, the Lord turns to Adam and rebukes him (vv. 17–19).

It is right after all this that the Bible says in verse 21, "the LORD God made for Adam and for his wife garments of skins and clothed them." And then sadly, the Lord removes Adam and Eve from the garden. We will come back to why God removed them from the garden in a second.

But notice how God graciously doesn't fix their problem.

If you understand the effectiveness of God's grace to be that He fixes your problems, then you will likely live in a state of continual letdown with Him. Because—given the period of time in which we are living in, affected by sin nature—grace isn't intended to fix problems. Instead, it is intended to provide a way to dwell with God in the midst of problems.

Until Jesus returns, it is more likely that the problem will have to run its course.

Why?

Because sin and the effects from sin have to run their course.

In light of this, what does God do?

He clothes you.

He comforts you.

Apparently, the fig leaves weren't good enough for Adam and Eve. So, what does God do? He clothes them with "garments of skins" (Gen. 3:21).

This was God's way of graciously caring for Adam and Eve before they were to leave the garden. This design and purpose behind grace stands alone as beautiful and spiritually profound as, much later in the Bible, we will be clothed again; but this time we are clothed with God Himself, with Christ's righteousness (Gal. 3:27).

And one day, when Jesus returns, we will be clothed once more, but this time with immortality and imperishability (1 Cor. 15) so that we might live with God forever . . . without any of the effects of sin and sin nature.

More on this later in Part Three.

One final thought before this chapter ends: Right after God clothes Adam and Eve, He removes them from the garden.

Why?

I thought this book was about grace, you're thinking. That doesn't sound like a very gracious thing for God to do.

The Bible describes, "Then the LORD God said, 'Behold, the man has become like one of us in knowing good and evil'" (Gen. 3:22). This sounds similar to Genesis 1:26–27 when it said, "Then God said, 'Let us make man in our image, after our likeness.'"

So, what's the problem?

When God created mankind, it was never with the intention of the male and female being equal with God. They were always to remain the creature in relationship with their Creator.

But Satan tricked them, deceived them into thinking that if they ate from the fruit of the tree of the knowledge of good and evil they would become like God (Gen. 3:5). By eating the fruit, they demonstrated their desire to be more than merely a creature. They wanted to be just like God.

Because of this, the Bible says,

"Now, lest he reach out his hand and take also of the tree of life and eat, and live forever—" therefore the LORD God sent him out from the garden of Eden to work the ground from which he was taken. He drove out the man, and at the east of the garden of Eden he placed the cherubim and a flaming sword that turned every way to guard the way to the tree of life. (Gen. 3:22–24)

God removed Adam and Eve from the garden so that something even worse didn't happen.

What are you talking about? you might be wondering.

Sin is in the world. Adam and Eve now suffer from all the effects of sin nature. Including their eventual physical death. They just took the life of an animal and clothed themselves with its skin. Then they are removed from the garden. And this isn't the worst part?

What could be worse than that?

What would be worse is if Adam and Eve in this condition were to eat from the tree of life and live in that sinful condition forever.

Instead, God's grace will have to be enough.

It was enough before the Fall. It will be enough after the Fall.
God has a gracious plan. But in the meantime, His grace will be enough.
Grace will always be enough.

Interlude: Jonah, the Son of Truth

What follows next in Part Two are three examples where God's grace endures our sinfulness. And what we will discover is that even in the midst of our sinful condition, God provides the sacred space for us to dwell with Him. Our first example comes from the prophet Jonah.

CHAPTER 14

You Can Run

Jonah is a very short book in the Bible.

There are other short books too, but let's just say this one is awkwardly short.

Awkward?

Yes.

Why?

Because of how it abruptly ends.

The book just stops in the middle of God asking a question.

The last verse in Jonah reads, "And should not I pity Nineveh, that great city, in which there are more than 120,000 persons who do not know their right hand from their left, and also much cattle?" (Jonah 4:11).

The end.

Isn't there some rule that says you shouldn't cut God off in the middle of saying something?

See I told you, it's awkward.

And of all things, God ends talking about cattle?

But what about the beginning of the book? Surely that has to be more detailed.

Not really.

Jonah begins similar to how it ends. Abruptly.

It says, "Now the word of the LORD came to Jonah the son of Amittai" (Jonah 1:1). All we gather from the first verse is that someone named Jonah receives a word from the Lord, and that he is the son of Amittai.

Could this have something to do with grace?

Let's explore this.

Jonah's name means "dove," which in the Bible is a name for someone you love. For example, in the Song of Solomon the one beloved in that story is called "my dove" (Song 2:14).

Why is that significant?

If Jonah had a biblical reputation, I wouldn't describe it as positive. For starters, he's famous for getting swallowed by a huge fish because of his disobedience. Then later he gets mad at God because he didn't get what he wanted.

Yet the Bible wants you to know that Jonah is God's dove. Jonah is beloved.

We also discover that Jonah is the son of Amittai. In Hebrew, Amittai is closely related to the word truth. In other words, Jonah is the son of truth.

Thus, in the first verse we are introduced to God's beloved dove, the son of truth.

This is meaningful because Jonah is going to expose a not so loving side of himself. On top of that, Jonah is also going to reveal a deep misunderstanding of God's grace.

That God is the giver of grace. Not Jonah.

After Jonah is introduced to the reader, God then commands him to "arise, go to Nineveh, that great city, and call out against it" (Jonah 1:2). God was sending Jonah to the Ninevites, so that they might turn from their wicked ways. The Lord even describes how "their evil has come up before me" (v. 2).

Thus far, other than the sudden beginning, everything is stereotypical to other prophetic books in the Bible.

However, after the Lord commissions Jonah, this son of truth responds to the Lord in a not so typical way. He refuses to go. The Bible says, "But Jonah rose to flee to Tarshish from the presence of the LORD" (v. 3).

Jonah flees, and what he runs from is very specific—the "presence of the LORD."

In the Hebrew the word "flee" (*bārah*) is a fairly common word in the Old Testament and in most of its almost thirty occurrences it refers to one fleeing from an enemy, or a compromising location or situation. For example, the Israelites fled from Pharaoh in Egypt. But here Jonah isn't fleeing from a dangerous location or an enemy. Instead, Jonah is fleeing from "the presence of the LORD."

Let that sink in.

Grace makes it possible to flee from the presence of God.

Grace does what?

I wouldn't say it's a good option, or recommended, but it's a possibility, nonetheless.

If I could only count how many times I've met pastors who tell me they would have gotten into ministry much earlier if they had listened to God. Instead, they describe a feeling as though they were running from God and their calling. And people have different reasons for fleeing from God. Perhaps they have a good job and don't feel they can give that up. Or perhaps they are fearful of the dreaded thought, *What if God calls me to be a missionary in Africa?!*

The reasons are many, but the result is the same—they ran from God.

What about you?

It isn't just pastors or people in full-time ministry who run from God. What is the small whisper within your heart drawing your attention to? You're probably telling yourself, "I'll do that one day. But I first have to make sure my family is taken care of." Or maybe you're thinking, "I'll do that one day when I am retired."

Following the Lord can be scary. As a result, sometimes we run. But God is sovereign, which means you won't overcome God's will by disobeying or avoiding your calling. God's grace is patiently waiting for you, maybe even giving you the space to run.

For me it was teaching. There was a time when I was absolutely terrified to get in front of people and talk. My hands would sweat. My knees would shake. My mouth would feel like I hadn't drunk water in weeks. As a result, every time I was asked to teach, I would politely say, "No, thank you." To be honest, that feeling hasn't totally gone away, and to this day, I still get a little scared.

Sometimes what God calls us to is linked with our fears.

I know, brutal right?

When a Christian tells me they are afraid of talking in front of people, or they get nervous sharing the gospel with strangers, I immediately begin to wonder if the Lord is calling them to do that very thing.

Why?

Because the Lord is clearly putting something on their heart; in this case they are thinking about what it would look like to teach God's Word or share the gospel with complete strangers. Something they wouldn't normally do. And their immediate response to the Lord is no. Spiritual gifts require faith and obedience. And yet, on the other side God receives glory as you bless the body of Christ with your spiritual gifts.

Wouldn't it be great if your spiritual gifts were connected to your comfort? How fun would that be? What if, when God called me to teach, my initial response was "Great! I love speaking in front of people."

In that moment I would step right in, prepared and ready to serve.

Sounds good, right?

As good as that might sound, we would likely never be dependent on God's help to understand the spiritual gift because we could figure it out on our own.

When God calls you, He is calling you to dependency on Him—dependency with Him to understand the task or gift at hand.

Back to my question. What are you fleeing from?

The next time you find yourself called, even drawn, deep down to a spiritual gift, yet you avoid it and run because you are terrified, pay attention to that, because it isn't random at all. Nothing with the Lord is random.

The Lord might just be revealing a spiritual gift and maybe even a specific way He wants you to use that gift.

Back to Jonah. What was he running from?

CHAPTER 15

Jonah Knows the Truth

One of the truths we wrestled with in the last chapter is that we can run from God.

However, when we run from God that doesn't mean we've tricked or overcome God's sovereignty in those moments. Instead, it is only by God's grace that we have the ability to flee from Him.

What's fascinating is that even while running from God's presence, Jonah never questioned who God is.

Jonah knows the truth.

Instead, Jonah is running away from God's presence *because* he knows who God is.

More specifically, he knows the truth about God's grace.

It's not enough to simply say Jonah fled from God's presence spiritually; he literally ran away. The Bible describes how "he went down to Joppa and found a ship going to Tarshish. So he paid the fare and went down into it, to go with them to Tarshish, away from the presence of the Lord" (Jonah 1:3).

Then the Lord "hurled" a great wind.

This was intense. Such a severe wind that it caused the experienced sailors to think that the boat was going to "break up" (v. 4).

Understandably, the sailors were terrified. Out of fear, their response was that everyone on the ship was to call out to their god for help (v. 5).

The sailors didn't know where to find truth. They weren't the son of Amittai.

But no god responded.

The sailors then began to throw cargo and anything heavy into the sea to lighten the ship (v. 5).

Then the captain remembered Jonah and he found him sleeping in the "inner part of the ship" (v. 6).

Sleeping?

The ship is being tossed and turned and about to break into pieces. The sailors are convinced they are going to die, and what is Jonah doing?

Sleeping.

Jonah is at rest in the middle of this storm because he knows who God is.

But, you're thinking, I thought rest was found as we are dwelling with God . . .

Yes.

What do you do when you know the truth? You rest in God's truth.

But what if Jonah knows exactly who is behind the storm at hand? In other words, what the sailors perceive as a fierce storm, Jonah understands in whose presence he is dwelling.

Once the captain finds Jonah, he admonishes him to call out to his god. The captain even wonders, "Perhaps the god will give a thought to us, that we may not perish" (Jonah 1:6).

Then the sailors decide to cast lots, "that we may know on whose account this evil has come up on us" (v. 7). And the lot fell on Jonah. Then a series of questions follow:

"What is your occupation? And where do you come from? What is your country? And of what people are you?" (v. 8).

At every turn the sailors and captain have no idea what the truth is.

They don't know whose god can save them.

They don't know where the storm came from.

They don't know who caused the storm.

They don't know anything about Jonah.

And yet, Jonah knows the truth. And what do you do when you know the truth? You rest in God's truth. In Jonah's case, you sleep. And if I were Jonah, sleeping isn't a bad idea considering he has a busy few days ahead of him. We'll get to that.

After this interrogation from the sailors and captain, Jonah responds to their questions; the dove tells them the truth. "I am a Hebrew, and I fear the LORD, the God of heaven, who made the sea and the dry land" (Jonah 1:9). It is never in question as to whether (or not) Jonah knows who God is.

Think about this: Even though Jonah is running from God's presence he still describes how he fears the Lord. He knows who God is, the Creator of everything, including the sea, which is hurling this great wind against them.

And picture this: While Jonah is saying this the storm is still raging.

Jonah's response to the crew is, "I am a Hebrew, and I fear the LORD, the God of heaven, who made the sea and the dry land."

We know who the Creator is.

We know who made the sea and dry land.

Remember?

It was Jesus.

He is the Creator of all things (Col. 1; John 1), and He is also the one who upholds all things through the power of His word (Heb. 1).

Even storms are not outside of Christ's providential care for His creation.

Earlier we looked at the Gospels, when another storm occurred. In that storm also, Jesus is sleeping.

Just like Jonah.

During that storm the people are also freaking out.

Just like the sailors and captain.

In the Gospels, Jesus speaks to the storm, and it calms down. What's amazing isn't that the storm listens to Jesus merely because He is God. Rather, the storm is listening to its Creator and Sustainer. Thus, when the Creator says calm down, the winds listen.

Back to Jonah.

Knowing that something wasn't right and that someone on the ship was not in favor with God, they cast lots to see who is responsible. The lot fell on Jonah (Jonah 1:7–8).

In response they said, "What is this that you have done!" (v. 10).

Jonah then tells them more of the truth. That he is "fleeing from the presence of the LORD" (v. 10).

Not knowing what to do, they asked Jonah, who said, "Pick me up and hurl me into the sea; then the sea will quiet down for you, for I know it is because of me that this great tempest has come upon you" (v. 12).

The men didn't listen because they believed this would be a death sentence for Jonah, so they attempted to row back to the shore. It didn't work though, as the storm only grew in its intensity (v. 13).

> God's grace is intended to endure our desires to flee from His presence.

Then "they picked up Jonah and hurled him into the sea, and the sea ceased from its raging" (v. 15).

The storm stopped.

Can you imagine Jonah's head bobbing in the now calm water and he's looking at the sailors and captain as if, "See, I told you"?

As a result of everything they had just experienced, here's how the Bible describes the aftermath of the scene: "Then the men feared the LORD exceedingly, and they offered a sacrifice to the LORD and made vows" (v. 16).

Then the "LORD appointed a great fish to swallow up Jonah. And Jonah was in the belly of the fish three days and three nights" (v. 17).

The Bible says the Lord "appointed."

This is important.

Jonah has fled from God's presence, and yet all along the Lord is in complete control.

The Lord is the one who caused a great storm to hurl upon the ship. And now the Lord has appointed a great fish to swallow Jonah.

This begins to awaken us to another reality, that even though we think we are able to flee from His presence, by God's grace we can't.

The creature is never able to flee from its Creator.

Instead, God's grace is intended to endure our desires to flee from His presence.

CHAPTER 16

Amazement

The second chapter in Jonah is a little misleading.

Why?

Because when you first read it, you think Jonah has finally come to his senses and is going to repent of his sin.

Instead, something different happens.

Right after Jonah is swallowed by a "great fish," the Bible tells us that he is in the belly of the fish for three days and three nights (Jonah 1:17).

Stop for a moment.

As Christians, anytime we read about three days and three nights, it should remind us of another three days and three nights in the Bible.

Do you remember which one it is?

It has to do with Jesus and His death, burial, and resurrection.

It has to do with the gospel.

In 1 Corinthians 15:3–5 we get perhaps one of our clearest explanations of the gospel. It says, "For I delivered to you as of first importance what I also received: that Christ died for our sins in accordance with the Scriptures, that he was buried, that he was raised on the third day in accordance with the Scriptures, and that he appeared to Cephas, then to the twelve."

Thus, Christ's death, burial, and resurrection give a unique Christian meaning to three days and three nights.

That's why even though Jonah 2 doesn't allude to the coming Messiah or mention Jesus specifically, as Christians we can't help but see Jesus in the story.

Moreover, when Jesus read Jonah, He even saw Himself.

Apparently, there was a time when the scribes and Pharisees asked Jesus for a sign (Matt. 12:38). Jesus responds to them this way: "An evil and adulterous generation seeks for a sign, but no sign will be given to it except the sign of the prophet Jonah. For just as Jonah was three days and three nights in the belly of the great fish, so will the Son of Man be three days and three nights in the heart of the earth" (Matt. 12:39–40). Then Jesus goes on to say, "Something greater than Jonah is here" (v. 41).

Who was greater?

It was Jesus.

Jonah emerged from the belly of the fish after three days and three nights, yet Jesus was telling the scribes and Pharisees that He would emerge from the grave. He would rise from the dead.

By the way, do you think Jonah was actually swallowed by a great fish? Or do you just think this was just a story used to illustrate God's love and grace in His redemptive plan?

You might think I am crazy. But I believe this story is real. I believe Jonah was real. That the sailors and captain were real. I believe Nineveh was a real place. I believe Jonah fled to Tarshish, a real location. And I believe God appointed a great fish to swallow Jonah. I believe Jonah survived and prayed to God from the belly of the fish. I also believe the fish vomited Jonah up after three days. We will get to the vomiting part in the next chapter.

Why do I believe this is real?

Because as a Christian there are all kinds of things I believe that seem crazy.

I believe in the Trinity, that God is one being, eternally existent as three persons.

I believe in the hypostatic union, that Christ is one person with two natures—a fully divine nature and a fully human nature.

I believe that God created everything from nothing.

I believe that the Bible is the inspired and inerrant Word of God in the original manuscripts.

These are just a few things that I believe as a Christian. That's why the thought that a great fish might swallow a man for a few days and spit him out doesn't shock me. If it did, then I have other more crazy things I need to address first.

Here is another question—similar, but different.

Why do I believe Jonah being in the belly of the fish for three days and three nights is important?

Did you notice what Jesus did in Matthew 12:38–42? He said that the Son of Man will be in the heart of the earth for three days and three nights, just like Jonah was in the belly of the fish. If Jonah was merely a mythical story, we need to understand how that will then affect our belief in the death, burial, and resurrection of Christ. They are directly linked together. Jesus ties them together. Why would Jesus connect the resurrection to a fake story? To believe in the gospel is crazy—and remember, I'm okay with crazy. Just like believing Jonah was in the belly of the fish is crazy.

> If Jonah was merely a mythical story, we need to understand how that will then affect our belief in the death, burial, and resurrection of Christ. They are directly linked together. Jesus ties them together.

Let's get back to Jonah.

While in the belly of the fish Jonah prays, and his prayer is such that he acknowledges God's constant presence in his life. It wasn't in the moment the prayer took place that Jonah is brought into the presence of God. Rather, Jonah is declaring that even when he was fleeing from the presence of God (Jonah 2:1–9), there is a gentle faithfulness on the part of God to remain with him. For Jonah, this is amazing.

After reading this prayer a few times I've yet to see where Jonah repents of his sin. Instead, it's more of a prayer of amazement.

Even though Jonah knew this truth, he was experiencing the reality of this truth sitting in the belly of the fish. There really is no place he can go where God is unable to find him or hear him. That is what is so amazing about God's grace. It gave Jonah the sacred space to flee, but never from God's presence.

This scene echoes the psalmist:

Where shall I go from your Spirit?
    Or where shall I flee from your presence?
If I ascend to heaven, you are there!
    If I make my bed in Sheol, you are there!
If I take the wings of the morning
    and dwell in the uttermost parts of the sea,
even there your hand shall lead me,
    and your right hand shall hold me.
If I say, "Surely the darkness shall cover me,
    and the light about me be night,"
even the darkness is not dark to you;
    the night is bright as the day,
    for darkness is as light with you. (Ps. 139:7–12)

The relationship we have with God is such that He has graciously granted us permission to flee, but not from His gracious presence.

We will get to what it looks like to return to God a little later.

But for now, I'm wanting us to sit in this truth, that after the Fall, man's natural response is to run from God. And what these first two chapters of Jonah awaken within our hearts is the reality that God is always there.

His grace is waiting for us every time we stop to take a breath and plot our next move.

CHAPTER 17

Who Knows?

After Jonah finished praying, the Bible describes how the Lord "spoke to the fish, and it vomited Jonah out upon the dry land" (Jonah 2:10).

In a very short book, this is the third time God displays His raw sovereignty.

The first was through a storm "hurled" upon the sea (Jonah 1:4).

The second was "appointing" a fish to swallow Jonah (Jonah 1:17).

Third, the Lord again speaks to the fish, resulting in Jonah being vomited on the dry land.

What we can't miss is that in the midst of Jonah's disobedience, the Bible never lets our attention get too far before reminding us that God is the one hurling and appointing and speaking to His creation.

And notice how creation obeys its Creator.

What happens next is that the word of the Lord comes to Jonah again, saying, "Arise, go to Nineveh, that great city, and call out against it the message that I tell you" (Jonah 3:2).

This command from God sounds very similar to what He said at the beginning.

Here are these verses next to each other:

Jonah 1:2 says, "Arise, go to Nineveh, that great city, and call out against it, for their evil has come up before me."

And Jonah 3:2 says, "Arise, go to Nineveh, that great city, and call out against it the message that I tell you."

One might ask, "Why is God repeating Himself?"

What if what God had originally said to Jonah was good enough? There is no need to say something different. The only difference is that this time Jonah listens. This time Jonah goes to Nineveh as the Lord had said.

While in Nineveh, Jonah performs his prophet duties, the Bible says that he spoke to anyone who would listen, "Yet forty days, and Nineveh shall be overthrown!" (Jonah 3:4).

Thankfully the people of Nineveh listened and believed God (v. 5). The Bible describes how there was great humility among the people of Nineveh, and that they "called for a fast and put on sackcloth, from the greatest of them to the least of them" (v. 5).

Jonah's message of repentance reached all the way up to the king of Nineveh. The Bible depicts a scene in which the king rose from his throne and "removed his robe, covered himself with sackcloth, and sat in ashes" (v. 6).

Not only that, but the king also issued a decree: "Let neither man nor beast, herd nor flock, taste anything. Let them not feed or drink water, but let man and beast be covered with sackcloth, and let them call out mightily to God. Let everyone turn from his evil way and from the violence that is in his hands" (vv. 7–8).

Then the king of Nineveh said, "Who knows? God may turn and relent and turn from his fierce anger, so that we may not perish" (v. 9).

What does he mean by "Who knows?"

I've got a story about that.

Last summer Lolly asked if I could stay with Carson, so that she could take Kaden and Oliver to vacation Bible school.

I said, "Of course!" Carson was sleeping and I was getting some writing done at the dining room table.

While everyone was upstairs getting ready to go, I heard Carson start to cry and then heard Lolly go into his room. Immediately in my head I thought, *Oh, she is getting Carson now that he is awake and taking him with her.*

Not too long after they left, I took a break from writing. The house was quiet, and I remembered that Lolly had asked me to clean the dining room table because "this table is for eating, not for books."

But then I thought, "These books can't be put away because they haven't been stamped yet."

Haven't been stamped yet?

Yes!

If you have a new book, before you put that book on the shelf, you have to give it the personal stamp showing it's yours.

It's a real thing.

Some of you know exactly what I am talking about.

The only problem was I needed more ink for my stamp. Then I had the best idea. I would run to Hobby Lobby real fast, get the ink, get home and start putting the books away. Lolly would love that!

I got in the car, drove a short distance down the road to Hobby Lobby, and bought the ink.

On my way home Lolly sent me a text, which read: "How is the babe? Is he awake?"

Is he awake?!

I texted her back and said, "I don't know, I'm on my way home from Hobby Lobby!"

She immediately wrote me back and said, "Are you serious?!"

I said, "Yes! I thought you took him with you when he woke up and cried!"

She said, "Kyle! Get home!!"

In that moment my heart relocated to my stomach. Not because I was afraid for Carson. I was afraid for my life.

I thought, "Who knows" how she will kill me. "Who knows" when she will talk to me again. "Who knows" how long she will be mad at me.

Clearly leaving your eighteen-month-old at home isn't ideal. But I was confident he would be okay. He was likely still asleep. And if he was awake, he couldn't get out of his crib. At least this is what I was telling myself.

Now I am racing home. And so is Lolly.

All I am thinking is that I have to get home before she does. I don't know why, but that felt right. Then I make the turn onto our road, and I see Lolly just making the turn. I was going to beat her home.

I get in the house and immediately listen for the baby.

Nothing.

Then I hear a whimper.

Then Lolly walks in the door—well, runs in the door. She runs upstairs and is gone for a while.

> She said, "Do you know how much grace I am giving you right now?" I said, "A lot. Thank you!"

Lolly doesn't say anything the whole time. No text messages. Nothing. It's killing me.

Then she comes downstairs with the baby and I thought, "This is it."

She turns the corner and faces me with Carson and says in this sweet voice, "Daddy left you all alone, buddy! Can you believe it?"

All I remember thinking was, *I'm going to live!*

I took a chance and smiled and said sorry to Carson and Lolly about my stupidity. And she said it's fine.

Then she said, "Do you know how much grace I am giving you right now?"

I said, "A lot. Thank you!"

A little later I got a text from my good buddy. "So how was watching Carson this morning?"

Cat was out of the bag. I'm never going to be able to live this down.

Think of the most intimate relationship in your life. The person you are the closest to. For me it's my wife. Lolly is my favorite everything and best friend. But here is the thing—in order for our marriage to work in a fallen world, we have to extend grace to each other. And each time you extend grace to one another, and forgive each other, what you are doing is testing "Who knows?"

The Bible also uses marriage to illustrate the intimate relationship Christ has with the church. In fact, the church is even called the bride of Christ. However, where this marriage analogy breaks down is that sometimes our human grace is unable to mend the relationship. For example, this could be physical, verbal, or emotional abuse, or adultery, sexual immorality, or other terrible things that no one should ever go through. Whereas with God, there is never a scenario in which His grace is unable to forgive and restore our relationship with Him.

Once we understand how God intended grace, then we begin to know the answer to the king's question of "Who knows?"

God's grace often leaves us wondering.

Who knows if God will forgive me?

Who knows if God will still love me?

And yet, "Who knows?" becomes one of our most complex theological questions, and it's the grace of God that forms the basis for our answer. As God forgives us again . . . and again . . . and again.

Even when you leave Carson home alone.

CHAPTER 18

Because You Are Gracious

The people of Nineveh, from the least to the greatest, turned from their evil ways. As a result, God relented "of the disaster that he had said he would do to them" (Jonah 3:10).

This story is finally beginning to make a turn for the better, right?

Well, what happens next is a strange response from Jonah.

The Bible describes that Jonah was displeased and angry (Jonah 4:1).

Why?

The people responded to his message of repentance. God forgave them and relented from the disaster he had warned them about. This is the best-case scenario playing out right in front of Jonah.

And he's displeased?

And angry?

Then Jonah prays: "O Lord, is not this what I said when I was yet in my country? *That is why* I made haste to flee to Tarshish; for I knew that *you are a gracious God* and merciful, slow to anger and abounding in steadfast love, and relenting from disaster. Therefore now, O Lord, please take my life from me, for it is better for me to die than to live" (vv. 2–4).

What has been clear from the start is that Jonah wanted to run away from God's presence.

That's a significant move because God's presence encompasses all of who He is.

Let's think about this. Jonah never had a problem with God being sovereign (Jonah 1:4). Jonah never had a problem with God being the Creator of the dry land and sea (Jonah 1:5). Jonah never had a problem with prayer and talking to God (Jonah 2). Jonah never doubted God's ability to forgive (Jonah 3:4–5).

What then is Jonah running from?

Jonah says, "For I knew that you are a gracious God."

That is why Jonah fled to Tarshish.

We finally know why.

It has to do with grace.

Jonah knew that if he were to go to Nineveh and preach a message of salvation and if the people responded and turned from their wicked ways, that God would lavish grace upon them.

This bothered Jonah.

So much so, Jonah ran away. He ran in the complete opposite direction. According to Jonah, this was the only way he could prevent God's grace from being misused.

Thus, it isn't enough to simply say that Jonah is fleeing from God's presence. We have to be more specific; by fleeing from God's presence, what Jonah is doing is attempting to withhold the presence of God's grace from the Ninevites.

Yet God wouldn't allow Jonah to thwart His plan and desire to graciously forgive Nineveh.

Jonah is a story about the grace of God.

Do you remember what word God used to describe Nineveh?

Two times God tells Jonah to "arise, go to Nineveh, that *great* city" (Jonah 1:2; 3:2).

In God's eyes, Nineveh is "great."

Nineveh is worth saving.

But for Jonah, if God were to forgive Nineveh this wouldn't be so great. As Christians, we can relate to this. It almost feels as though there is a spiritual injustice when God's grace is used to forgive another sinner.

However, if we're honest, any relationship with God is an injustice. Whether you have murdered someone, or whether you have committed the most heinous of sins, or whether you happen to be the most holy person in the world. Because we are sinners, affected by sin nature, to have a relationship with God requires us to be dependent on grace in order to dwell in God's presence.

If you think about it, the same theology applies to each stage of redemptive history. Adam and Eve did nothing to deserve a relationship with God prior to the Fall, we have done nothing to deserve a relationship with God after the Fall, and in the new heaven and new earth, we'll have done nothing to take credit for once we receive our glorified bodies and step foot into an eternal relationship with God.

Grace makes everything possible.

This means that we are never to overlook another due to their sinfulness. Never to conclude that God doesn't want a relationship with them.

There is never a scenario in which someone's sin is greater than God's ability to forgive them of that sin. To do so would be to claim that someone's sin is greater than God's grace, which is an even greater injustice.

Instead, we bring a message of grace and forgiveness to the world, which says, whoever believes in the Lord will not perish, but have eternal life (John 3:16).

That's the good news.

But this goes beyond salvation. This also means that as Christians, we are never outside God's ability to forgive. That we are always welcomed back home. That God takes great delight when one of His children turns their heart back toward the Lord once again. And when they do, God is ready to forgive them.

There is another passage in the Bible that talks about God's beloved.

123

First John 4:7–12 says,

> *Beloved*, let us love one another, for love is from God, and whoever loves has been born of God and knows God. Anyone who does not love does not know God, because God is love. In this the love of God was made manifest among us, that God sent his only Son into the world, so that we might live through him. In this is love, not that we have loved God but that he loved us and sent his Son to be the propitiation for our sins. *Beloved*, if God so loved us, we also ought to love one another. No one has ever seen God; if we love one another, God abides in us and his love is perfected in us.

Here's the thing, even though this passage says nothing about Jonah. What if we replaced the word "beloved" with the name Jonah? After all, he is God's beloved dove.

"This is love, not that we have loved God but that he loved us."

If we did that, the passage would read like this,

"*Jonah*, let us love one another, for love is from God, and whoever loves has been born of God and knows God. Anyone who does not love does not know God, because God is love. In this the love of God was made manifest among us, that God sent his only Son into the world, so that we might live through him. In this is love, not that we have loved God but that he loved us and sent his Son to be the propitiation for our sins. *Jonah*, if God so loved us, we also ought to love one another. No one has ever seen God; if we love one another, God abides in us and his love is perfected in us."

John admonishes Jonah, I mean Christians, to love one another.

But why?

Because love is from God.

Because God is love.

Which means that when someone does not love, according to John, this means they don't know God. But Jonah does. He knows the truth. He even told God so much when he explained why he fled to Tarshish. He said, "For I knew that you are a gracious God and merciful, slow to anger and abounding in steadfast love" (Jonah 4:2).

Abounding in what?

Steadfast love.

John says, "In this the love of God was made manifest among us, that God sent his only Son into the world, so that we might live through him. In this is love, not that we have loved God but that he loved us and sent his Son to be the propitiation for our sins" (1 John 4:9–10).

John appeals to the way in which God's grace endured our sinfulness on the cross. Because God loved us, for this reason we ought to love one another. Because God has extended grace to us, we ought to be gracious toward one another.

John continues, "No one has ever seen God; if we love one another, God abides in us and his love is perfected in us" (1 John 4:12). This is fascinating. John is saying that because God is invisible, that means we can't see Him. However, when we love one another, when we are gracious toward one another, we actually make God visible.

This is how serious Jonah's refusal was. By refusing to go to Nineveh, Jonah was withholding God from the Ninevites.

He was withholding God's presence.

He was withholding God's grace.

The next time we are angered with God's grace being used to forgive a sinner, may we remember that we are the grace of God that people experience. Which means when we withhold grace and run, people actually think God is running from them.

God never runs away.

If anything, He runs *to* us. More on that later.

But when we press in and love them and extend grace, they experience not human grace. They experience God.

Grace bothers Jonah.

As Christians, we must make sure it doesn't bother us.

CHAPTER 19

Jonah Needs Just as Much Grace

After God extends grace to the Ninevites, Jonah leaves the city. Not because his job is done.

Rather, Jonah leaves because he's angry that God "relented of the disaster that he had said he would do to them" (Jonah 3:10).

The Bible describes how Jonah sat on the east side of the city and made a booth for himself there so that he might have some shade (Jonah 4:5).

Then what happens next is more grace.

See, the booth that Jonah created outside the city wasn't good enough.

How do I know that?

Because God graciously appoints a plant that immediately grows up high enough to provide shade for Jonah to comfortably dwell under (Jonah 4:6). So high that it overshadows Jonah's creation.

Looking back, this sounds eerily similar to God's reaction to the clothing Adam and Eve made for themselves after the Fall.

Remember what God does?

He clothed them with something better (Gen. 3:21).

The booth Jonah made wasn't good enough either.

So what does God do?

Even while Jonah was sulking in anger, God's desire was for him to be comfortable (v. 6). Thus, God provided shade through His appointed plant, which made it possible for Jonah to rest in his anger.

Rest in his anger?

This doesn't even sound right.

Yet, if you think about it, God already provided the gracious space for Jonah to run from His presence.

Then the Bible says something interesting: "But when the dawn came up the next day, God appointed a worm that attacked the plant, so that it withered. When the sun rose, God appointed a scorching east wind, and the sun beat down on the head of Jonah so that he was faint" (vv. 7–8).

Here we go again—God sovereignly appoints more. This time it's worms and intense heat. As a result, the plant that was providing shade withers away.

> Jonah's problem is that he wants to not only deliver God's message of grace and forgiveness, but he also wants to be the one who determines who receives it.

It is almost like God gave Jonah the day to be angry. It's like God was saying, "You know better, you know the truth. You're the son of truth." But instead, Jonah still steeped in his self-loathing as he requests to die outside the city in the heat (v. 8).

Then God said, "Do you do well to be angry for the plant?"

To which Jonah replies, "Yes, I do well to be angry, angry enough to die" (v. 9).

This plant isn't just a plant. Instead, God is using it to illustrate to Jonah that God is the one who gets to determine who gets shade and who doesn't. In terms of grace, God is the only one who gets to determine who receives His grace and who doesn't.

Jonah's problem is that he wants to not only deliver God's message of grace and forgiveness, but he also wants to be the one who determines who receives it.

But that isn't his responsibility.

God is trying to help Jonah see that this isn't how grace works.

That God is the one who gives His grace to whomever He wants.

Even to the Ninevites.

Let's get back to the plant.

The plant withers and dies and Jonah gets angry (Jonah 4:9).

He's very dramatic.

The Lord responds to Jonah with, "You pity the plant, for which you did not labor, nor did you make it grow, which came into being in a night and perished in a night" (v. 10).

Think grace.

The plant was a gracious gift that Jonah had nothing to do with. It's like God is saying, "I graciously gave you the plant when you didn't deserve it. You enjoyed this plant and now you become angry when I take it away?"

Then the story ends.

Just ends?

Yes, the last verse, Jonah 4:11 just says, "And should I not pity Nineveh, that great city, in which there are more than 120,000 persons who do not know their right hand from their left, and also much cattle?"

Done.

End of story.

But why does Jonah have a problem with God's grace?

I'm sure there are a lot of reasons, but I think one big reason is that Jonah was never fully aware of the ways in which God had extended grace to him.

Throughout this whole story we've seen a childish prophet complaining and running from God because the Lord wants to bestow grace on Nineveh.

Again, why does Jonah have such a problem with this?

I think it's because Jonah hasn't fully accepted that God has done the same for him.

In other words, Jonah thinks he is better than the Ninevites.

The gospel of Matthew provides a helpful illustration as to why Jonah has a problem with God's grace.

There was this time when the Pharisees approached Jesus trying to trick him (Matt. 22:35). The goal was to catch Jesus saying something wrong so that then they could have a charge to bring against Jesus and His followers.

A Pharisee asked,

> "Teacher, which is the great commandment in the Law?" And he [Jesus] said to him, "You shall love the Lord your God with all your heart and with all your soul and with all your mind. This is the great and first commandment. And a second is like it: You shall love your neighbor as yourself. On these two commandments depend all the Law and the Prophets." (Matt 22:36–40)

Jesus' response was that the most important thing one might do is actually an action that originates from the heart. It is to love. To love God and your neighbor.

For our purposes though, here's a phrase worth considering. What does Jesus mean by "love your neighbor *as yourself*" (v. 39)?

As yourself?

Why not just say, "And a second is like it: You shall love your neighbor"? Why add the "yourself"?

Because you can't love your neighbor without first knowing that you are graciously loved by God.

And for Jonah, he doesn't know how to love the people of Nineveh because he doesn't know how to love himself and accept the grace that God has given him.

If Jonah knew this, he would have run *to* Ninevah. Not away.

Interlude: The Prodigal Son

In Part Two we're considering three examples where God's grace endures our sinfulness. And what we will discover is that even in the midst of our sinful condition, God provides the sacred space for us to dwell with Him. We discussed Jonah. Now our second example of God's grace comes from the parable of the prodigal son.

CHAPTER 20

Grace Receives Sinners

Right in the middle of the gospel of Luke we step into some interesting family drama.

Jesus tells a story about a father who has two sons.

And what we find is God's heart toward those in need of grace.

Because this story in situated in the middle of the gospel (Luke 15:11–31), it will be helpful for us to gain some background for what is happening leading up to Jesus' parable of the prodigal son.

It's a moment when the Pharisees and scribes are grumbling, saying, "This man receives sinners and eats with them" (Luke 15:2).

This word "receives" (*prosdechetai*) is deeply relational.

Think companionship.

Think to welcome someone in a warm way.

Think to receive someone with hospitality.

In other words, what Jesus is doing is not repudiating the sinners but receiving them in a friendly manner.

The sinners likely already knew what the law said about their lifestyle or behavior. They also likely knew what Judaism or this new way of following Jesus had to say.

However, what was uncertain was whether (or not) someone would still love them.

Thus, Jesus enters their worlds, not to condone, but to befriend.

He chooses to dwell with them.

This is what grace does; it does not ignore or overlook sin, but rather grace meets us right where we are so that we might have a relationship with God.

Now it makes a little more sense why it bothered the Pharisees and scribes that Jesus would receive these people. They would never grace such people with their presence. And since they were the theological experts, they were certain God felt the same way.

Then as Jesus often does, He begins to tell stories.

And each of these parables serves to illustrate what it means to love people. Particularly those whom the religious elites have refused to love.

> This is what Christian love looks like. It's the ability to love those whom everyone else has rejected.

This is what Christian love looks like. It's the ability to love those whom everyone else has rejected. Christian love looks at the world and pays close attention to everyone who has been rejected and cast aside and decides in the name of Jesus to love them.

But why?

Because when we were unlovable, God graciously loved us.

Loving those who are easy to love does not distinguish Christian love from any other love. Jesus says, "For if you love those who love you, what reward do you have?" (Matt. 5:46). Jesus adds that even the tax collectors can do the same.

Christian love is determined by how well we love those that the world has deemed unlovable.

Then right after Jesus is questioned by the Pharisees and scribes about befriending sinners, Jesus tells a parable (Luke 15:4) about a man who loses one of his sheep. "What man of you, having a hundred sheep, if he has lost one of them, does not leave the ninety-nine in the open country, and go after the one that is lost, until he finds it?"

Those listening to Jesus would have been well aware of the correct answer. They would have left the ninety-nine in pursuit of the one lost sheep. And Jesus even describes that when the man returns with his once lost sheep, how his friends and neighbors join in rejoicing over finding this sheep (v. 6).

What's the point of this story?

It is intended to point the reader back to why Jesus even told the story in the first place.

The Pharisees and scribes were upset that Jesus would welcome sinners. That He would share a meal with them (v. 2). Yet Jesus goes on to say, "I tell you, there will be more joy in heaven over one sinner who repents than over ninety-nine righteous persons who need no repentance" (v. 7).

Jesus is spending time with these "sinners" that the Pharisees and scribes don't want to associate with. They want to tend to the ninety-nine righteous people, but Jesus would rather look for that one lost sheep.

God graciously spends His time looking and doesn't give up until He finds you.

Then Jesus tells another story, but this time about a woman who loses one of her ten silver coins. In this parable Jesus asks a question. He asks in Luke 15:8, "What woman, having ten silver coins, if she loses one coin, does not light a lamp and sweep the house and seek diligently until she finds it?"

The assumption for Jesus is that she will look everywhere. And when she finds the coin, just like the shepherd above, she will celebrate with friends and neighbors, saying, "Rejoice with me, for I have found the coin that I had lost" (v. 9).

Thus far, Jesus is stringing together a series of stories that are helping explain why it is that He would spend so much time with sinners. Why He would eat with them.

To the Pharisees, this seems like wasted time. Yet the grace of God never wastes time. Jesus then reaffirms, "I tell you, there is joy before the angels of God over one sinner who repents" (v. 10).

According to the Pharisees and scribes, righteous people do not entertain, nor associate with sinners.

Jesus wants to change this.

In another gospel, Jesus is described as sitting reclined at the table of a tax collector. Mark describes the scene like this: "Many tax collectors and sinners were reclining with Jesus and his disciples" (Mark 2:15). Just as before, the Pharisees and scribes were questioning this behavior from Jesus. "Why does he eat with tax collectors and sinners?" (v. 16).

There it is again.

Notice Jesus' response to the Pharisees and scribes this time. "Those who are well have no need of a physician, but those who are sick. I came not to call the righteous, but sinners" (v. 17).

God's grace is always interested in that one. The outcast. The lost. The sick. The vulnerable.

God's heart is always to find us.

Here's a question: Do you think Jesus didn't know where the lost sheep was?

Or how about the coin, do you think Jesus didn't know where it was?

Of course, He knew. He is God. He knows everything.

So why encourage them to keep looking until they are found?

Because we aren't Jesus.

We don't know what He knows. We don't know where the lost sheep are. We don't know where the lost coin is. But according to Jesus, that's okay. As Christians, the most effective way to find sinners to is receive them. To eat with them. To befriend them.

In other words, it is God's ministry to reveal where the good soil is.

The good soil?

Yes.

Earlier in the gospel of Luke is a scene in which a large crowd had gathered to hear from Jesus. The Bible says that people from town after town had traveled to hear from Him (Luke 8:4). Jesus told them a parable about a sower who went out into the field to sow seeds.

Jesus described how some of the seeds fell along the path, and the birds came and devoured them (v. 5).

Then Jesus told how some of the seeds fell on the rocky ground, "and as it grew up, it withered away, because it had no moisture" (v. 6).

Then Jesus depicted how other seeds fell among the thorns, and when the thorns grew up they choked the seeds, preventing them from growing (v. 7).

Finally, some of the seeds fell on the good soil and it "grew and yielded a hundredfold" (v. 8).

The disciples had no clue what Jesus was talking about and so they asked Him privately what the parable was about (v. 9). Jesus responds to the disciples and tells them that the seed is the "word of God" (v. 11).

Just like with the sheep and coin in Jesus' parables, we don't know where the good soil is.

In other words, the seed is Jesus Himself.

The seed is grace.

Jesus then explains the parable to the disciples. "The ones along the path are those who have heard; then the devil comes and takes away the word from their hearts, so that they may not believe and be saved" (v. 12). Then Jesus continues, "And the ones on the rocks are those who, when they hear the word, receive it with joy. But these have no root; they believe for a while, and in time of testing fall away" (v. 13).

Then He explains that "as for what fell among the thorns, they are those who hear, but as they go on their way they are choked by the cares and riches and pleasures of life, and their fruit does not mature" (v. 14).

Finally, the good soil. "As for that in the good soil, they are those who, hearing the word, hold it fast in an honest and good heart, and bear fruit with patience" (v. 15).

Why would He tell this story?

Because once again, we aren't Jesus.

Just like with the sheep and coin in Jesus' parables, we don't know where the good soil is.

But notice how Jesus' lesson to the disciples isn't how to find the good soil and then only sow seed there.

That would require a kind of knowledge only God possesses.

Think about it; if sinners had that kind of knowledge, it could be troublesome. Who knows? Maybe we'd become like Jonah and decide that Nineveh is not the good soil. That the sheep will never be found. And that we should give up looking for the coin.

Instead, Jesus' desire is to sow Him everywhere. Don't worry if the Word of God falls along the path, or on the rocks, or among the thorns. Don't bother yourself with things that God isn't worried about. God's grace is able to endure the elements, and ultimately, the seed will fall on the good soil. But we won't know where the good soil is until God reveals it to us.

That's why Jesus teaches the disciples to sow Him to everyone. That's why we are to leave the ninety-nine. And why we are to turn the house inside out looking for the coin.

It is God's ministry to reveal where the sheep and lost coin can be found, and where the good soil is. And until the Lord reveals, the disciples are to keep looking. The disciples are to keep sowing seed everywhere.

This is what it looks like to graciously receive sinners.

CHAPTER 21

It's Time to Go Home

We forgot to ask an important question in the last chapter.

At the beginning of Luke 15 the Pharisees and scribes were grumbling (Luke 15:2).

But *why* were they grumbling?

It sounds like they were upset at the attention Jesus was receiving. The Bible describes how "the tax collectors and sinners were all *drawing near* to hear him" (Luke 15:1). As a result, the religious leaders were unsettled and began to complain, saying, "This man receives sinners and eats with them" (v. 2).

Knowing how they felt, Jesus responds by telling "them" a few stories in order to illustrate what it means to receive sinners (v. 3). And "them" here is referring to everyone: the tax collectors, sinners, Pharisees, and scribes.

Do you remember what those stories were?

One was about a lost sheep (Luke 15:3–7), and the other was about the woman's lost coin (vv. 8–10). In both parables the owners drop everything and search until they are found.

I'm curious though; what does "drawing near" mean (v. 1)?

Because whatever is behind this word will shed light on what is bothering the religious leaders so much. And I'm always intrigued when something bothers the people who think they know it all. Especially when the subject matter is God.

To "draw near" (*eggizō*) in the Greek means to approach, or come near, or draw closer to oneself.

In other words, not only are these sinners drawing near to Jesus, but there is also the idea that He is stepping into their worlds and coming near to them. Moreover, in the New Testament, "drawing near" is a word often used to describe our relationship with God. For example, in James 4:8 it says, "Draw near (*eggizō*) to God, and he will draw near (*eggizō*) to you."

That is what happens when you experience God's grace.

It draws you near to Him.

It's something these sinners in Luke's gospel likely never experienced in their interactions with the religious leaders. No wonder the tax collectors and sinners are "drawing near" to Jesus.

But will some still accuse you of spending too much time with sinners? Unfortunately, yes.

Will some even blame you for condoning sinful behavior?

Probably.

You are in good company though, since at one point Jesus was even accused of being a drunk because He was spending so much time with sinners (Luke 7:34).

Let's go back to Luke 15, because Jesus isn't done. He has another gracious story to tell.

This story begins with "There was a man who had two sons" (v. 11).

And the younger of the two sons approaches his father and asks for his share of the inheritance (v. 12). In response, the father gives the son what he is asking for and divides his property between the two sons.

Notice that this son has received an inheritance, not based on anything he has done. In other words, the younger son has received, by grace, his inheritance as a gift.

It is also important to point out that even though the son asked for the inheritance, it was the father's decision to give it to him. The father was not coerced or forced against his will.

What then does the younger son do with this inheritance?

Jesus relates how "not many days later, the younger son gathered all he had and took a journey into a far country, and there he squandered his property in reckless living" (v. 13).

He spends it all. On all kinds of sinful things.

Jesus then describes that "a severe famine arose in that country" (v. 14) and the younger son was in bad shape. He had nothing. In order to survive, the son "hired himself out to one of the citizens of that country" and his job was to take care of the pigs (v. 15).

Jesus depicts this young man as being so tired and hungry that he was considering eating the food prepared for the pigs (v. 16). Yet somewhere along the line, probably as he is staring at the pig slop, the younger son realized that his father's hired servants have more than enough bread to eat (v. 17).

That's when he decided to go back to his father and that he would say to him, "Father, I have sinned against heaven and before you. I am no longer worthy to be called your son. Treat me as one of your hired servants" (vv. 18–19).

> **Grace is like the father's kisses and compassion, and waiting, and running, and embrace.**

Pause for a moment.

Do you remember how we found ourselves here?

The Pharisees and scribes had been grumbling, saying, "This man receives sinners and eats with them" (Luke 15:2). Then Jesus tells two stories, one about a lost sheep and the other about a lost coin. In both of these stories, when the sheep and coin are found, Jesus describes how there is great celebration in heaven over one lost sinner who repents.

Wouldn't it be something if the father received the son with rejoicing, just as the rejoicing over finding the lost sheep and lost coin?

The story continues as the son returns to the father, and Jesus says, "But while he was still a long way off, his father saw him and felt compassion, and ran and embraced him and kissed him" (v. 20).

This is what it looks like for God's grace to endure our sinfulness.

At some point along this journey you might've thought, "Why would God allow His grace to endure this?"

Here's why.

Because grace is like the father's kisses and compassion, and waiting, and running, and embrace.

The father graciously gave the son his share of the inheritance and the boy wasted it all. But that isn't the father's concern. The father is never worried about the money. The father is overjoyed that his son is home. He's come back. He's been found. Even though the son has squandered the father's grace, he has now returned to the father. And in order for this relationship to continue, the son will need more grace.

However, the father's embrace reveals the abundance of God's grace.

There is always more.

This means that for us, we can always go home. It may take a great deal of humility to return, but that humility will never be returned to you with humiliation.

Upon returning home, the son tells his dad,

"Father, I have sinned against heaven and before you. I am no longer worthy to be called your son." But the father said to his servants, "Bring quickly the best robe, and put it on him, and put a ring on his hand, and shoes on his feet. And bring the fattened calf and kill it, and let us eat and celebrate. For this my son was dead, and is alive again, he was lost, and is found." And they began to celebrate. (Luke 15:21–24)

God's grace was never intended to condone sin, but He did design grace to endure our sinfulness. Which means that grace does not allow the son to live in humiliation. God's grace does not result in shame.

In a fallen world, God's grace was intended for moments such as this.

Elsewhere in the New Testament it says, "Let us then with confidence draw near to the throne of grace, that we may receive mercy and find grace to help in time of need" (Heb. 4:16).

When one of God's children returns, His grace stands ready to receive them.

That's why Jesus eats with sinners.

The Pharisees and scribes don't understand this about grace; they think grace is only meant for righteous people. That the church is only meant for healthy people. They don't understand why anyone would look for one lost sheep when you have ninety-nine others. They don't understand why you would spend so much time looking for one coin when you have nine others.

That God's grace would endure our sinfulness means that this son is able to draw near to his father, and when he does, a celebration ensues.

CHAPTER 22

It's Okay to Celebrate

Up to this point in the story, the attention has largely been on the relationship between the younger son and his father.

And what we've observed is that the father's grace was more than ready to endure the sinfulness of his rebellious son.

We saw this in a few ways. First, the father graciously gave his son his inheritance as a gift, only to watch him waste it through "reckless living" (Luke 15:13).

Then when the son had nothing left, he returned home, not as a son, but hoping to be a hired servant in his father's house (vv. 17–19). However, even though the younger son returned in shame, the father refused to let the son remain in that humiliation. Instead, the father graciously received his son with kisses, and compassion, and running, and embrace.

Not only that, but the father threw a big party because his son has been found.

But what about the older brother?

What ever happened to him?

In Luke 15:25 we find the older brother "in the field, and as he came and drew near to the house, he heard music and dancing" (v. 25). This is interesting—get this, the older brother "drew near" to the house. This is the same word we talked about last chapter to describe how the tax collectors and sinners were "drawing near" (*eggizō*) to Jesus. Now in the story the older brother is the one drawing near.

I don't know if the older brother had FOMO (fear of missing out) or not, but this party didn't wait for him. The celebration commenced immediately, even while he was out in the field working.

The Bible says that the older brother asked one of his father's employees what was going on. To which the man replied, "Your brother has come, and your father has killed the fattened calf, because he has received him back safe and sound" (v. 27).

God's grace is meant to be received.

Remember Ephesians 2:8–9 from earlier? It says, "For by grace you have been saved through faith. And this is not your own doing; it is the gift of God, not a result of works, so that no one may boast." By God designing grace to endure our sinfulness, He is creating the necessary conditions for you to receive His grace as a gift.

And the more honest we are with our sin, the more we will appreciate that this happens over and over and over again. In order for sinful creatures to have a relationship with God in a fallen world, grace must endure our sinfulness. Otherwise, a relationship isn't possible. The father in this story is demonstrating before our eyes, that he is willing to receive his children when they return.

God's grace is a promise that He will receive you when you return.

But still, what about the older brother? Does he join in the celebration? Not exactly.

He becomes angry.

The older brother refuses to go to the party. Refuses to eat. Refuses to drink. And certainly, refuses to dance. Angry people don't dance. If the older brother could have fled to Tarshish he would have.

Aware that the older son refuses to come to the celebration, the father "came out and entreated him" (Luke 15:28). In the Greek, "entreat" (*parekalei*) means to invite someone in, or to be friendly to someone, or it can convey treating someone in an inviting manner.

In other words, the father is attempting to draw the older son near to the celebration.

Stop for a moment.

At the very beginning of Luke 15, what did the Pharisees have such a problem with? That Jesus was "receiving" sinners in a friendly manner. I love this—what Jesus is doing in this parable is telling the Pharisees and scribes that they are just like the older brother in this story.

Do you want to know how to tell if you are a pharisee?

If when a sinner repents and returns to God, you have a problem with that. If you are unable to celebrate what God's grace is able to accomplish. Then you are no better than the Pharisees. No different than Jonah. You are just like the older brother.

This younger son is the father's lost sheep. He is the father's lost coin.

What Jesus is saying is that we should celebrate such moments. We should join the angels rejoicing in heaven over "one sinner who repents" (v. 10). We should enjoy the fattened calf of God's grace because they have returned.

When the father comes out to entreat his older son, it isn't just to persuade him to join the party, but rather, the father is entreating his son to enjoy the father's grace. That it's okay to celebrate when one of God's children comes home.

God's grace is a cause of celebration.

CHAPTER 23

I'm the Older Brother

The older brother is not buying it; he's upset with the father and argues, "Look, these many years I have served you, and I never disobeyed your command, yet you never gave me a young goat, that I might celebrate with my friends. But when this son of yours came, who has devoured your property with prostitutes, you killed the fattened calf for him!" (Luke 15:29–30).

You can feel the injustice in the older brother's heart. You can hear the injustice in his voice. He feels like his little brother is getting away with murder. Taking full advantage of his father's grace.

In the gospel of Matthew we find a story that helps illustrate the heart of the older brother. Matthew 20:1 says, "For the kingdom of heaven is like a master of a house who went out early in the morning to hire laborers for his vineyard."

The master of the house agreed to pay the laborers one denarius a day (v. 2). Then we read that he saw some people standing in the marketplace looking for work, and so he hired them for—you guessed it—one denarius (v. 4).

Then a few hours later he did the same.

Then a few hours after that he did it again (vv. 5–6).

Essentially, the idea is that all throughout the day the master of the house keeps hiring people to work for him. Each getting paid one denarius. Whether you started working early in the morning, or late in the day, each got paid the same amount.

Now, at the end of the day, the master of the house called the people in so that they would be paid for their work. He specifically instructs the fore-man to pay them their wages beginning with the last (v. 8). This meant that the workers who had been there all day, faithfully working, had to watch those who barely got there before the day ended get paid one denarius.

God's generous grace toward us is that He never leaves us nor forsakes us, but desires to have a relationship with us.

As a result, the Bible describes the workers as grumbling, exactly like the Pharisees grumbled when Jesus received sinners (Luke 15:2). This time, the workers grumbled saying, "These last worked only one hour, and you have made them equal to us who have borne the burden of the day and the scorching heat" (Matt. 20:12).

This sounds eerily similar to the older brother, who said, "Look, these many years I have served you, I have never dis-obeyed your command, yet you never gave *me* a young goat, that I might celebrate with my friends" (Luke 15:29).

Both the older brother and the hired workers from earlier in the day feel the injustice. Their obedience and faithfulness have been overlooked, so they think, and this makes them mad.

Then in Matthew 20:13–15, the master of the house says, "Friend, I am doing you no wrong. Did you not agree with me for a denarius? Take what belongs to you and go. I choose to give to this last worker as I give to you. Am I not allowed to do what I choose with what belongs to me? Or do you begrudge my generosity?"

This is really what the older brother has a problem with; he has an issue with the generosity of the father's grace. He has a problem with the father's decision to give an equal amount of grace. It bothers him that there isn't a lesser grace to give to the younger brother.

And yet, the father gives the same grace to the younger brother on his return home. God's generous grace toward us is that He never leaves us nor forsakes us, but desires to have a relationship with us.

As Christians, we are no better than the Pharisees or the older brother when we are bothered by God's choice to allow His grace to endure sinfulness in order to save someone who is lost. Instead, the gospel—the good news—is that God's grace is enough.

It was intended to always be enough.

The father is always standing ready to welcome you. Even if some older brother or sister whom God also loves has a problem with it.

I honestly never knew how much God's grace enduring sinfulness bothered me.

But it does.

To be honest, writing this book has exposed a not so pleasing side of my heart. Here is what I have come to learn. What frustrates the older brother (i.e., me!) is that it appears like the father just allows His grace to be taken advantage of. He doesn't care about the party, or the drinks, or the food. It's the felt injustice when the younger brother receives the same grace that the older brother receives.

What's worse is that the older brother (a.k.a. me!) actually thinks deep down that he is better than the younger brother because he doesn't take advantage of the father's grace. That's why he said, "Look, these many years I have served you, I never disobeyed your command" (Luke 15:29).

However, the father, not the older brother, is the model for how we should love those around us, even those we feel are misusing God's grace.

The father is the one who is able to determine who receives his grace *and* how much of his grace is to be given. And what's unsettling to the older brother is that the father gives abundantly of his grace.

Thus, the story of the prodigal son is a gracious story. Not just gracious toward the runaway son, but also toward the older brother working in the field. In both instances, the father's grace endures sin for the purpose of a relationship.

Now, you might be thinking, I see where the younger brother has benefited from God's grace, but what about the older brother?

The older brother sins by refusing to welcome his brother home. By refusing to celebrate. This is not how you love someone. Thus, the father's grace endures the sin buried deep within the heart of the older brother.

In both instances, the father's grace endures the sinfulness of his children.

The major difference is the older brother doesn't think he has sinned and benefited from God's grace.

Too often, people are made to feel that we are a burden to God because His grace must once again endure our sinfulness.

Thankfully, the father, and not the older son, is the one who has the power and authority to give grace.

At the very end, the father simply replies, "Son, you are always with me" (Luke 15:31). Notice the dwelling language from the father. Then he continues, "And all that is mine is yours. It was fitting to celebrate and be glad, for this your brother was dead, and is alive; he was lost, and is found" (vv. 31–32).

Now this is a gospel message that we long to hear. Too often, people are made to feel like God doesn't want a relationship with them because of their sin. That we are a burden to God because His grace must once again endure our sinfulness. But that's not true. In those instances, people are reacting not to God, but to Christians. In other words, they are reacting to the older brother. Or to go all the way back to the beginning of Luke 15, they are reacting to the Pharisees (v. 2). Or to go back even further, they are reacting to Jonah.

No wonder sinners aren't drawing near.

Something we have to understand is that when the prodigal sons and daughters in our lives refuse to return home, that doesn't always mean they are rejecting God. They might just be avoiding their older brother. They might be rejecting the pharisee in their life. They know their older brother wants nothing to do with them, and as a result, they figure God feels the same way.

CHAPTER 24

Daughter of God

Lolly and I drink too much Starbucks. We always talk about cutting back and drinking coffee at home and then somehow end up going the next day.

One thing about going to Starbucks so often is that you get to know the people who work there.

You become a regular.

Not too long ago, I noticed there was someone new.

Her name was Luci.

What caught my eye was Luci's tattoo on her forearm: "Daughter of God."

And the "t" in "daughter" was depicted as a cross.

I told her, "I like your tattoo." Then asked, "Are you a Christian?"

She took her hand and slowly covered her forearm and said, "Oh thanks. I'm actually getting that one removed. It's not really my thing anymore."

It was a powerful moment as we looked at each other not sure what to say next.

Then I replied, "I know we don't know each other, so feel free to not answer this next question, but how did you get there?"

She thought for a moment.

Then Luci said, "I've just seen stuff. The church is no longer a safe place."

As she said this, we both realized the line was growing quite long, which meant that was where we had to leave it.

That day I left Starbucks different than how I walked in. My heart hurt for Luci. Even though I had no idea what happened to her, I was mad that church made her feel like that. Here was someone so in love with Jesus that she gets a tattoo on her arm for all to see that proclaimed her being a daughter of God. Then because of an experience (or maybe a number of experiences) Luci decides she no longer wants to be identified as a daughter of God.

But can you do that?

Can you just tell God *I don't want to be Your child anymore?*

And does God listen to that?

Would He really just give up on one of His children?

Then I got to thinking, well maybe she was never really a Christian in the first place. Maybe she was never really saved. But who gets a tattoo proclaiming to be a daughter of God, when in fact they weren't?

These questions all hinge on what you think about grace.

And I believe grace is powerful.

Like really powerful.

Maybe the most powerful thing in the whole universe.

When it comes to salvation, as Christians we are saved by our belief in the gospel. That means that nothing we have done has earned any favor with God or justified to God that we deserve to be saved. Instead, salvation is a gracious gift given by God to those who believe in the Lord Jesus. An important passage we've already mentioned is Ephesians 2:8–9, where Paul writes, "For by grace you have been saved through faith. And this is not your own doing; it is the gift of God, not a result of works, so that no one may boast."

Notice the beauty and simplicity as our relationship with God is described as a gift, thankfully not dependent on what we have done, but rather firmly established by grace.

Sounds pretty good, right? So, what's the trouble?

The problem is that you and I don't know what God knows. And spiritually, because we are sinners, one of the things we wonder about is if we are saved.

Was it just me or did you ever pray "the sinner's prayer" and ask Jesus into your heart a few extra times, just to make sure, in case it didn't work the first time? No? Just me?

By the way, just because you ask these types of questions doesn't mean you are a bad Christian. A lot is riding on the truthfulness of all this.

But what if we asked a slightly different question, which is, *How* are we saved by grace?

Are we supposed to do anything?

Or does God just notify us one day with the good news. "Congratulations, Kyle! You're a Christian! Please respond 'Yes' to confirm, or 'No' to opt out of these text messages in the future."

The apostle Paul is helpful here, and I don't mean with texting.

Paul says, "If you confess with your mouth that Jesus is Lord and believe in your heart that God raised him from the dead, you will be saved. For with the heart one believes and is justified, and with the mouth one confesses and is saved. For the Scripture says, 'Everyone who believes in him will not be put to shame'" (Rom. 10:9–11).

> It isn't just words that save you, but rather the words are an audible declaration of what the heart already believes.

According to Paul, one must confess a belief in the Lord Jesus in order to be saved. And this confession is rooted within what the heart already believes about Jesus. It isn't just words that are repeated that save you, but rather the words are an audible declaration of what the heart already believes.

For example, there was this time Paul and Silas were in Macedonia and because they were performing miracles and preaching the gospel, the authorities threw them in jail for disturbing the city (Acts 16:20–24).

Then at about midnight Paul and Silas were singing hymns and praying to God and all the prisoners were listening to them (v. 25). Suddenly there was a great earthquake! It was almost like God wanted to show what disturbing the city was really like. The Bible states that the very foundation of the prison was shaken (v. 26).

Then the Bible describes how immediately "all the doors were opened, and everyone's bonds were unfastened" (v. 26).

But Paul and Silas didn't run.

No.

They stayed (v. 28) and shouted to the jailer, "We are all here!"

The jailor came rushing in and found them still there, but the man was trembling. He was afraid of what he just experienced. The jailor then fell down before Paul and Silas and asked, "Sirs, what must I do to be saved?"

And Paul and Silas told him, "Believe in the Lord Jesus, and you will be saved" (vv. 30–31).

So how are you saved?

According to Paul, if you believe in your heart that Jesus is Lord, you will be saved. This is how powerful the grace of God is. God's grace was never intended to condone sin. Yet, grace has the ability to save you, even in spite of who you are and the sin you have committed.

Grace gives you the assurance and confidence to know in your heart that you are a child of God, and nothing can change that.

Nothing?

Yes.

Not only does the grace of God have the power to save you, but grace also has the capacity to secure you in God's hands no matter what. Jesus says, "My sheep hear my voice, and I know them, and they follow me. I give them eternal life, and they will never perish, and no one will snatch them out of my hand" (John 10:27–28).

That means that grace secures the relationship God shares with His child so that nothing can remove them from the hand of God.

Which makes sense, if we have done nothing to earn our salvation, then why would God suddenly then give us the ability to un-earn our salvation?

But what about some Christians? Because of the way they live their lives, we wonder if they were ever really saved.

Or maybe for whatever reason someone decided after years of following Christ that they no longer want to be a Christian.

Is this person saved?

Honestly, I don't know.

My lack of confidence here isn't due to a belief that people can lose their salvation. My hesitancy is related to my inability to know things as God does. But I do know what grace is. And nothing in the universe is more powerful than grace.

That means when we are dealing with the question of whether (or not) someone is *really* saved, it is a speculative question from our human perspective. Only God knows with certainty if they ever really believed in Jesus.

> God's grace saves and secures the believer in a relationship with Himself.

For the purposes of our conversation, let's just say that God comes down and tells us, yes, Luci is saved. Yes, she believed in the Lord Jesus. Then, based on what we know about grace, we know that God saves us and secures us as His own.

She is a daughter of God.

And thanks to grace, Luci hasn't done anything to earn her salvation, and to be consistent, she also can't do anything to un-earn her salvation. Even if she attempts to remove the label "daughter of God" from her body.

Surely someone reading this right now is having a spiritual panic attack that Luci is saved. They are convinced that because she has renounced her faith in Jesus that somehow, she was never really saved in the first place.

But notice what I am grounding my conclusion on.

It is grounded on the belief that God's grace saves and secures the believer in a relationship with Himself. I am not promoting a sinful lifestyle. I'm not supporting that one should renounce their faith. I am simply saying that there is no sin greater than God's ability to secure our relationship with Him. Remember, in this scenario it was God, not anyone else, that confirmed that Luci believed in the Lord Jesus.

Now, on the other hand, what if instead God tells us Luci did not believe. She was never really saved. With that, we would then be able to remove the mystery and know with certainty that even though she tattooed "daughter of God" on her arm, she was never a believer.

If that is true, then technically Luci didn't lose her salvation because she was never saved by grace.

Here is the thing, I don't know if Luci ever believed in Jesus.

God has never shared that with me.

He doesn't need to either.

But I'm confident in how powerful grace is.

Who knows? One day Luci might find out too.

Interlude: The Passion of Christ

In Part Two are three examples where God's grace endures our sinfulness. And what we will discover is that even in the midst of our sinful condition, God provides the sacred space for us to dwell with Him. Our third example of God's grace comes from the passion of Christ.

CHAPTER 25

Even Judas' Feet

Feet gross me out.

Because my kids are well aware of this, they always try and get Dad to kiss their feet when they're "hurt."

Oliver is notorious for this.

Somehow, even if he falls on his knees or shoulder or back, he will immediately roll over and say, "My foot! Daddy, it hurts so bad!" And of course, when Lolly offers to kiss his foot that won't work.

As a result, I pick up his foot and get really close and give it a good air kiss. To which Oliver will say, "Daddy, no right here!" Pointing to his gross big toe.

Then I pick his foot back up and give it a quick kiss. This of course immediately heals Oliver, and he is off and running and wrestling with his brothers once again.

Meanwhile, I walk away feeling like I just kissed a frog.

Did you know there is a story in the Bible about Jesus and grace and feet?

At the beginning of John 13 we find Jesus with His disciples before the Feast of the Passover (John 13:1). The Bible says that Jesus "knew that his hour had come to depart out of this world to the Father" (John 13:1).

John also tells us that Jesus knew other things; for example, he knew that the devil was put "into the heart of Judas" to betray Him (John 13:2).

This is important because John wants the reader to know right from the start that Jesus is completely aware of what's going on.

Knowing this, what does Jesus do?

Does He get really weird around everyone?

Does He avoid Judas?

No.

Instead, Jesus *draws near*.

John writes that Jesus "rose from supper," and put His outer garments to the side (John 13:4). Then Jesus took a towel, tied it around His waist, and poured water into a basin and began washing the disciples' feet (v. 5).

Peter was confused. "Lord, do you wash my feet?"

To which Jesus responds, "What I am doing you do not understand now, but afterward you will understand."

Then Peter pushed back, "You shall never wash my feet."

Only to hear Jesus respond with, "If I do not wash you, you have no share with me."

To which Peter then exclaimed, "Lord, not my feet only but also my hands and my head!" (vv. 6–9).

Then Jesus said, "The one who has bathed does not need to wash, except for his feet, but is completely clean. And you are clean, but not every one of you" (v. 10).

"Not every one of you" is clean?

This is probably in reference to Judas, because remember Jesus "knew who was to betray him" (v. 11).

Then something subtle, but gracious happens. "When he had *washed their feet* and put on his outer garments and resumed his place, he said to them, 'Do you understand what I have done to you?'" (v. 12).

But what's so gracious about that?

Whose feet did Jesus just wash?

"Their" feet.

Who is "their" feet?

The disciples' feet.

Which included Judas. The one who would soon hand Him over to the authorities. And remember, Jesus knew this about Judas *before* He washed "their" feet.

This is yet another example of what grace enduring our sinfulness looks like. It's one thing to wash the feet of those you love, but it's a whole different thing to wash the feet of your enemy.

Yet Jesus is preparing the disciples for when He is gone (John 13:1). He is showing the disciples how they are to love one another. Could you wash the feet of someone you knew was going to betray you?

After Jesus had washed their feet, He put on His outer garments and sat back down (v. 12).

Then Jesus continued, "Do you understand what I have done to you? You call me Teacher and Lord, and you are right, for so I am. If I then, your Lord and Teacher, have washed your feet, you also ought to wash one another's feet. For I have given you an example, that you also should do just as I have done to you" (vv. 12–15).

The disciples have no clue yet.

They have no idea that Jesus has just cared for and washed the feet of His eventual betrayer.

However, the night isn't over, and Jesus isn't done talking to the disciples. He says, "Truly, truly, I say to you, a servant is not greater than his master, nor is a messenger greater than the one who sent him. If you know these things, blessed are you if you do them. I am not speaking of all of you; I know whom I have chosen" (vv. 16–18).

Stop.

Jesus said, "I am not speaking of all of you; I know whom I have chosen." What does that mean?

It means, Jesus knows what Judas is about to do. He knows everything. He is God. However, the magnitude of the moment for the disciples will come later when they realize that Jesus drew near to Judas and washed his feet.

Then Jesus said, "But the Scripture will be fulfilled, 'He who ate my bread has lifted his heel against me.' I am telling you this now, before it takes place, that when it does take place you may believe that I am he" (v. 18).

Jesus is quoting Psalm 41:9, which says, "Even my close friend in whom I trusted, who ate my bread, has lifted his heel against me." Jesus is explaining to the disciples that this verse from Psalm 41 is about Judas and Himself.

After saying all these things, John describes how Jesus' demeanor changed, and he writes, "Jesus was troubled in his spirit." Then Jesus said, "Truly, truly, I say to you, one of you will betray me" (John 13:21).

The disciples are now confused and shocked. They looked around at one another, "uncertain of whom he spoke" (v. 22). Then Peter asked the disciple whom Jesus loved (the apostle John) to ask Jesus, "Lord, who is it?" (v. 25).

Jesus answered, "It is he to whom I will give this morsel of bread when I have dipped it" (v. 26).

Jesus is not only teaching them with His words, but also through His actions.

Then Jesus dipped the bread and gave it to Judas (v. 26).

Then the Bible describes that "Satan entered into him" (v. 27).

And Jesus tells Judas, "What you are going to do, do quickly" (v. 27).

Then John writes, "Now no one at the table knew why he said this to him" (v. 28).

Notice how all the other instances of "knew" thus far in John 13 have been in reference to Jesus. But here, at the end of the story, "no one at the table knew" (v. 28). John simply writes that "some thought that, because Judas had the moneybag, Jesus was telling him, 'Buy what we need for the feast,' or that he should give something to the poor" (v. 29).

The scene ends with, "So, after receiving the morsel of bread, he immediately went out. And it was night" (v. 30).

Then after Judas left the room, Jesus instructs His disciples that they are to love one another. He says, "A new commandment I give to you, that you love one another: just as I have loved you, you also are to love one another.

By this all people will know that you are my disciples, if you have love for one another" (John 13:34–35).

In this moment, Jesus is not only teaching them with His words, but also through His actions. By washing their gross feet. Even the very feet of the one who would betray Him.

This is a powerful scene between Jesus and the disciples.

The magnitude of the event is that they don't know yet which one of them is going to betray Jesus. Only Peter and John know. The rest of the disciples are just sitting with the reality that it could be them. They are humbled by the thought that Jesus just washed their dirty feet.

Then imagine later when they witness Judas betray Jesus. I'm sure some of the disciples breathed a sigh of relief that it wasn't them. Then I bet their minds raced back to the upper room when Jesus washed Judas' feet and how He told them that they are to love one another as He has loved them.

The love that Jesus offers and calls His disciples to can only be offered through grace.

It doesn't make sense that Jesus would love Judas.

And yet that is the example Jesus chose to illustrate what it means to love one another.

That not even Judas is outside of God's ability to love.

Grace makes the most radical kind of love possible.

CHAPTER 26

What Is Truth?

In the last chapter we witnessed Jesus graciously washing the feet of the disciples in the upper room as they celebrated the Passover.

Now we meet Jesus again, but this time in a garden.

John writes, "When Jesus had spoken these words, he went out with his disciples across the brook Kidron, *where there was a garden*, which he and his disciples entered. Now Judas, who betrayed him, also knew the place, for Jesus often met there with his disciples" (John 18:1–2).

Apparently, Jesus spent a lot of time in gardens.

Remember how our journey first began?

It was in the garden of Eden.

Back when things were the way they were supposed to be. Before the Fall. Before grace was ever to endure our sinfulness. Jesus was there with Adam and Eve in that garden too. And everything was good. It was perfect.

However, what is going to take place in this garden isn't good, as Jesus will soon be handed over to the authorities to be tried and eventually crucified.

John describes how things unfolded. "So Judas, having procured a band of soldiers and some officers from the chief priests and the Pharisees, went there with lanterns and torches and weapons" (John 18:3). Their intention was to find Jesus.

John writes in verse 4, "Jesus, knowing all that would happen to him, came forward and said to them, 'Whom do you seek?'"

Notice how John once again is making us aware that Jesus knows everything.

They said, "Jesus of Nazareth."

Jesus then said to them, "I am he" (v. 5).

Then John goes out of his way to make sure that we know that "Judas, who betrayed him, was standing with them" (v. 5). Which means, the moment Jesus had predicted concerning Judas would take place (John 13:21–30) now happens.

Then something strange occurs. The men "drew back and fell to the ground" (John 18:6).

Then Jesus asked again, "Whom do you seek?"

They said again, "Jesus of Nazareth" (v. 7).

Jesus said, "I told you that I am he. So, if you seek me, let these men go" (v. 8). He was talking about His disciples. This was to fulfill Jesus' earlier prediction that none of His disciples will be lost (John 17:12).

Then Peter, in the middle of this intense moment, grabs his sword and strikes the servant to the high priest and cuts his ear off (John 18:10). John doesn't record this in his gospel, but in Luke's gospel we learn that Jesus rebukes Peter and says, "No more of this!" And then Jesus touches the servant's ear and heals him (Luke 22:51).

But in John's gospel (John 18:11), Jesus tells Peter, "Put your sword into its sheath; shall I not drink the cup that the Father has given me?"

In other words, "Peter, are you really going to stop Me from undergoing the cross?"

The answer is no.

Jesus knew He was to endure the cross so that we might have an eternal relationship with God.

After they captured Jesus, the first place they take Him is to Annas, "the father-in-law of Caiaphas, who was the high priest that year" (John 18:13). While before Annas, Jesus is questioned about His teachings.

Jesus explains, "I have spoken openly to the world. I have always taught in synagogues and in the temple, where all Jews come together. I have said nothing in secret. Why do you ask me? Ask those who have heard me what I said to them; they know what I said" (vv. 20–21).

This didn't go well, because when He had finished explaining Himself, one of the officers standing by hit Jesus in the face, saying, "Is that how you answer the high priest?" (v. 22).

This is the first instance during the passion of Christ where Jesus physically withstands abuse.

Then Jesus responds in verse 23, "If what I said is wrong, bear witness about the wrong; but if what I said is right, why do you strike me?" What Jesus is saying is remarkable because if what He said was indeed wrong, then technically, Jesus would be rightly punished for lying before the high priest. But he's not wrong. He's telling the truth.

After this exchange Annas sends Jesus bound to Caiaphas the high priest (v. 24).

John describes how it is "early morning" (v. 28) and Jesus is in the governor's headquarters. However, before meeting with Jesus, Pilate goes outside to meet with the Jewish religious leaders and asks, "What accusation do you bring against this man?" (v. 29).

> "What is truth?" Pilate has no idea how profound that question is. The truth is standing right before him.

Pilate then recommends that the Jewish religious leaders take Jesus and judge Him by their own laws (v. 31). But the religious authorities said, "It is not lawful for us to put anyone to death" (v. 31). This was to fulfill the prophecy that Jesus was to die in a very specific way (v. 32).

Crucifixion.

We read about what comes next in John 18:33–38. Then Pilate goes back into his headquarters to meet with Jesus. He asks, "Are you the King of the Jews?"

Jesus answered, "Do you say this of your own accord, or did others say it to you about me?"

Pilate says, "Am I a Jew? Your own nation and the chief priests have delivered you over to me. What have you done?"

Then Jesus said, "My kingdom is not of this world. If my kingdom were of this world, my servants would have been fighting, that I might not be delivered over to the Jews."

Pilate responds, "So you are a king?"

Jesus answers, "You say that I am a king. For this purpose, I was born and for this purpose I have come into the world—to bear witness to the truth. Everyone who is of the truth listens to my voice."

Then Pilate asks this question, "What is truth?"

Pilate has no idea how profound that question is.

The truth is standing right before him.

Pilate is looking at the truth with his own eyes.

He is listening to the truth with his own ears.

Jesus is the truth.

Earlier in the gospel of John, Jesus describes Himself as "the way, and *the truth*, and the life" (John 14:6).

Pilate is asking, "What is truth?"

And the answer can only be known by grace.

The answer is incarnational as Jesus has come down and dwelt among us so that we might dwell with God forever.

The answer to Pilate's question is Jesus.

Pilate then leaves Jesus and goes back outside to the Jews and tells them, "I find no guilt in him" (John 18:38).

He's innocent.

Yet according to custom Pilate is to release one man for the Jews at Passover (John 18:39). Pilate asks if he should release the "King of the Jews" (v. 39).

The Jews cried out, "Not this man, but Barabbas!" (v. 40).

This is grace. The convicted robber gets the gracious gift of life. The guy that actually broke the law is set free.

Yet Jesus, who has done nothing wrong, is sentenced to death.

John wants the reader to understand that Jesus is innocent. He isn't about to die because He has done something wrong.

This was the plan all along.

CHAPTER 27

It Is Finished

This is the moment.

In humanity's story, this is the climax of God's grace enduring our sinfulness.

Just as a warning though. It's graphic, and sad, but the more we sit with what Jesus went through on the cross, I believe the more thankful we become for the gift of God's grace. And the relationship we share with Him.

Our story continues in the gospel of John, where we learn that immediately after Pilate released Barabbas (John 18:39–40), he then took Jesus and "flogged him" (John 19:1).

Then "the soldiers twisted together a crown of thorns and put it on his head and arrayed him in a purple robe" (v. 2). This both mocked Jesus and was physically painful. The soldiers continued to ridicule Jesus by saying, "Hail, King of the Jews," and as they were chanting this, they hit Jesus with their bare hands (v. 3)!

However, before bringing Jesus out to the religious authorities, Pilate comes to them and says, "See, I am bringing him out to you that you may know that I find no guilt in him" (John 19:4).

Remember Pilate's earlier question, "What is truth?"

Pilate is beginning to realize the answer to his own question.

Then Jesus is brought out before the Jews, He was wearing the crown of thorns and the purple robe.

Pilate said to them, "Behold the man!" (John 19:5).

When the chief priests and officers saw Jesus, they cried out, "Crucify him, crucify him!" (v. 6).

But Pilate refused. "Take him yourselves and crucify him, for I find no guilt in him" (v. 6).

The Jews answered Pilate and said, "We have a law, and according to that law he ought to die because he has made himself the Son of God" (v. 7).

This freaked Pilate out.

The Bible describes Pilate as "afraid" (v. 8).

And fear here isn't merely in reference to killing an innocent man. Pilate is afraid that he is about to oversee the death of the Son of God (vv. 7–8).

As a result, Pilate went back to Jesus and asked, "Where are you from?"

But Jesus remained silent (v. 9).

Then in response to Jesus' silence, Pilate said, "You will not speak to me? Do you not know that I have authority to release you and authority to crucify you?"

Then Jesus responded, "You would have no authority over me at all unless it had been given you from above. Therefore he who delivered me over to you has the greater sin" (vv. 10–11).

It is almost like Jesus was comforting Pilate from the guilt he felt.

Then the Bible says from that point on Pilate sought to release Jesus (v. 12).

When the Jews saw that Pilate was beginning to waver and attempting to release Jesus, they cried out, "If you release this man, you are not Caesar's friend. Everyone who makes himself a king opposes Caesar" (v. 12).

Once Pilate heard this, he brought Jesus out "and sat down on the judgment seat at a place called The Stone Pavement, and in Aramaic Gabbatha" (v. 13). And he said to the Jews, "Behold your King!"

Now, I used to think that Pilate was just part of the problem. That he was mocking Jesus, like the soldiers when they put the crown of thorns on His head and yelled, "Hail, King of the Jews!" (John 19:3).

But I see things a little differently now.

I actually think that Pilate has the answer to his question, "What is truth?" Jesus is the truth.

He is the King.

And so, Pilate declared to the Jews, "Behold your King!"

After Pilate presented Jesus to the Jews, they cry out, "Away with him, away with him, crucify him!"

Pilate replied, "Shall I crucify your King?"

The chief priests answered, "We have no king but Caesar" (v. 15).

Pilate then delivered Jesus over to them to be crucified (v. 16).

The Bible then says that "they took Jesus," who was carrying His own cross, to "the Place of a Skull" (vv. 16–17). In Aramaic this place is called Golgotha. This is where they crucified Jesus, along with two other men, one on each side (v. 18).

At this point Luke records something that John doesn't. While Jesus was between the two criminals, Luke records that one of the men being crucified with Jesus said, "Jesus, remember me when you come into your kingdom" (Luke 23:42).

Then Jesus says, "Truly, I say to you, today you will be with me in paradise" (Luke 23:43).

This is a stunning moment in the story of God's grace.

The Greek word for paradise (*paradeisōs*) also means "the garden of Eden."

Jesus was telling this sinner that he would dwell with Him in the garden. Just like it was supposed to be.

Then John describes how Pilate wrote an inscription on the cross; it read, "Jesus of Nazareth, the King of the Jews" (John 19:19).

When the Jewish religious leaders read this the chief priests of the Jews said to Pilate, "Do not write, 'The King of the Jews,' but rather, 'This man said, I am King of the Jews'" (v. 21).

Pilate answered, "What I have written I have written" (v. 22).

In other words, the question is no longer, "What is truth?"

Instead for Pilate it is now, "This is truth."

When the soldiers had crucified Jesus, they took for themselves his garments and divided them into four parts (John 19:23). One for each soldier. However, Jesus' tunic was seamless, woven in one piece from the top to bottom, so in order to keep it in one piece they cast lots for the tunic (v. 24). This was to fulfill Psalm 22:18, "They divide my garments among them, and for my clothing they cast lots."

Then the Bible describes the scene around the cross, and thankfully Jesus was not alone. Jesus' mom was there. So was Mary's sister and Mary Magdalene (John 19:25). John, the disciple whom Jesus loved, was standing nearby too (v. 26). There was a sweet exchange as Jesus was enduring the cross when He looked at John and His mom. And He told John to look after and accept Mary as his own mother (v. 27). Jesus loved His mom.

The death of Christ is the greatest example of what it means for grace to endure our sinfulness.

After all this, Jesus knew that everything was now finished. He said, "I thirst," and near Jesus was a jar full of sour wine, so they put some on a sponge and held it up to His mouth to drink (v. 29). This was to fulfill another psalm: "They gave me poison for food, and for my thirst they gave me sour wine to drink" (Ps. 69:21).

After Jesus had drunk the sour wine, He said, "It is finished," and He bowed His head and died (John 19:30).

It is finished.

What is finished?

The abuse is over.

The work Christ accomplished on the cross was once and for all a forgiveness for our sins (Heb. 7:27). Jesus took upon Himself our sins "on the tree, that we might die to sin and live to righteousness" (1 Peter 2:24). God's grace was never intended to condone sin, but He did intend grace to endure our sinfulness. The death of Christ is the greatest example of what it means for grace to endure our sinfulness. There will never be a time in which Christ will undergo this kind of punishment on our behalf again. By His wounds we have been healed (Heb. 9:26). Now a relationship with God is possible forever (Rom. 5:10; Heb. 9:12).

This is a gracious thing.

In other words, it is finished.

PART THREE

Grace in the New Heaven and New Earth

Introduction to Part Three

In order to get to this point in the book we've traveled through some very important moments throughout human history. And what we've come to learn is that God has always had a gracious plan to dwell with us.

We started in the beginning, literally where it all began in Genesis 1:1.

We looked at how God graciously brought forth everything in order to have a relationship with us. This was the way things were supposed to be.

But everything changed.

In one moment: when Adam and Eve ate of the tree of the knowledge of good and evil (Gen. 3:6).

After the Fall things would be different. Life with God is now not the way it was supposed to be. In other words, grace would for the first time endure our sinfulness so that we might have a relationship with God.

In order for us to reconcile the idea that grace could withstand sin, we looked at the prophet Jonah and the parable of the prodigal son. Both of these stories illustrated that even with our best efforts, sin could not prevent God from having a relationship with us. *And* grace was God's chosen means to provide the way back to Him.

Finally, we spent time exploring the most powerful example of God's grace enduring our sinfulness.

The cross.

The moment when God offers Himself as a substitute for our sin, in order to establish an eternal relationship with Him. Paul writes, "All this is from God, who through Christ reconciled us to himself and gave us the ministry of reconciliation; that is, in Christ God was reconciling the world to himself, not counting their trespasses against them, and entrusting to us the message of reconciliation" (2 Cor. 5:18–19).

Then remember what Jesus said right before He died?

He declared, "It is finished."

His abuse was over.

Never to be repeated.

And what we will discover is that in just a few days, Jesus will reveal more as to what He actually accomplished when He triumphs over death through His resurrection.

That is what Part Three is all about.

We'll look at three biblical examples that illustrate how grace triumphs over our sinfulness.

This includes events like the new heaven and the new earth, and our hope rooted in the promise of our bodily resurrection when Jesus returns. But first, we will look at Jesus' resurrection in the gospel of John. This will be our first example of what it means for the grace of the Lord Jesus to triumph over sin.

CHAPTER 28

Garden of Grace

After Jesus declared, "It is finished," John tells us that Jesus "bowed his head and gave up his spirit" (John 19:30).

Then John describes how it was the "day of Preparation," which meant for the Jewish religious leaders that bodies could not remain on the cross on the Sabbath. Thus, they asked Pilate that their legs might be broken so that they could be taken away (v. 31).

But why break their legs?

Because the only way people who were crucified could stay alive is by pushing up on the nails so that they could take a breath.

Push up on the nails?

Yes.

One of the nails was pierced right through their feet.

Can you imagine the pain?

But the Jewish religious leaders didn't have time for these men to breathe. They needed to get this over with so that they could observe their religious "high day" (John 19:31). The soldiers then came through and broke the legs of the two men on either side of Jesus. That meant they were still barely alive, but not for long. Then they got to Jesus, but because He was already dead, they never broke His legs. But just to make sure He was dead one of the soldiers pierced Jesus' side with a spear and at once blood and water came out (v. 34).

Is there significance to this?

Yes.

These two events fulfill what was said about Jesus earlier in the Bible. The first is from Psalm 34:20, which predicts that His bones will not be broken: "He keeps all his bones; not one of them is broken." And the second is from Zechariah 12:10, which predicts that His side will be pierced. "And I will pour out on the house of David and the inhabitants of Jerusalem a spirit of grace and pleas for mercy, so that, when they look on me, on him whom they have pierced, they shall mourn for him, as one mourns for an only child, and weep bitterly over him, as one weeps over a firstborn."

Wait, God is going to pour what out on David and the inhabitants of Jerusalem?

A spirit of grace.

John then proclaims that this proved that the testimony was true and that "he is telling the truth" (John 19:35).

> **Here is the most important question you'll ever need to answer. Who do you believe Jesus is?**

I'm sorry to do this again, but remember Pilate's question to Jesus before He was crucified?

Pilate asks Jesus, "What is truth?"

It's Jesus.

Jesus is the way, *the truth*, and the life (John 14:6).

Here is the most important question you'll ever need to answer.

Who do you believe Jesus is?

After all these things take place we are introduced to a man named Joseph of Arimathea. John tells us that Joseph is a disciple of Jesus, but in secret, "for fear of the Jews" (John 19:38). Can you blame him after everything he had seen take place with Jesus?

Joseph asked Pilate if he could take away the body of Jesus, for which Pilate gave him permission (v. 38). Now, you might disagree with me, but I don't think Pilate was a bad guy. The Bible doesn't say anything about this, but I think Pilate believed Jesus was the King of the Jews.

John also tells us that Nicodemus had come to pay his respects to Jesus by night. And that he brought with him a large mixture of myrrh and aloes for His body (v. 39). Then they took the body of Jesus and "bound it in linen cloths with spices, as is the burial custom of the Jews" (v. 40).

Then John explains that near where Jesus was crucified there was a garden, and in the garden was a tomb in which no one had been buried (v. 41).

John said, "They laid Jesus there" (v. 42).

In the garden.

This is beautiful.

Where does humanity's story begin?

In a garden.

Where does humanity's story take an awful turn?

In a garden.

Where does God remove Adam and Eve from as a result of sin?

From a garden.

Where did God's grace first overcome our sinfulness?

In a garden.

Where did Judas betray Jesus?

In a garden.

Where did Jesus tell the criminal on the cross He would take him?

To paradise. Or to say it another way, to the garden of Eden.

Where did they bury Jesus?

In a garden.

And now, three days later where is God's grace going to triumph over sin?

In a garden.

CHAPTER 29

Grace Defeats Death

Early in the morning on the next day, Mary Magdalene came to Jesus' tomb. John describes that Mary got there so early it was still dark. As she approached the tomb, she noticed that the stone had been taken away (John 20:1).

Startled, she immediately ran back to Peter and John and explained, "They have taken the Lord out of the tomb, and we do not know where they have laid him" (v. 2).

Then right in the middle of a highly emotional moment, we see a little of the competitive nature of John.

Competitive?

Yes.

The Bible says that after Mary told Peter and John about the stone being moved, they ran back to the tomb to see for themselves what had happened. Then John describes how "both of them were running together, but the other disciple outran Peter and reached the tomb first" (v. 4).

John was the "other disciple," and he clearly wants you to know he ran faster.

Once they got to the tomb, they saw with their own eyes that Jesus was gone. What they witnessed was the linen cloths lying there and the wrap that was covering Jesus' face was "folded up in a place by itself" (v. 7).

That's a strange detail.

Have you ever wondered why the wrap covering Jesus' face was so nicely folded up?

Remember where we found the first instance of grace in the Bible?

"In the beginning God created [grace] the heavens and the earth" (Gen. 1:1).

Through creation God graciously gave us everything.

Do you remember who was responsible for creation?

Jesus.

Remember from Hebrews and Colossians that Jesus was the one responsible for creation? For example, "For by him [Jesus] all things were created, in heaven and on earth, visible and invisible, whether thrones or dominions or rulers or authorities—all things were created through him [Jesus] and for him [Jesus]" (Col. 1:16).

And in Hebrews it describes how Jesus "created the world" (Heb. 1:2).

Not only that, but Jesus is also the Sustainer and upholder of His creation (Col. 1:17).

Which means there is a reason why the sun and moon and the stars stay in their places. There is a reason why the ocean has its tides. There is a reason why Jesus brings order and calms the storm.

With Jesus there is orderliness to creation.

Theology has a word that describes the harmony and design and order behind creation. It's called the teleological argument: Creation itself is evidence that there is an intelligent and purposeful designer.

But what does this have to do with Jesus' folded-up face wrap in the empty tomb?

Even in the resurrection there is order.

God's grace was never intended to condone sin, but He did design grace to endure our sinfulness, and triumph over it.

This means with grace there is order and design.

When God triumphs over sin, He does so with purpose and intelligence and order and design. Even to the smallest detail, like folding up your face wrap before you leave the tomb.

Then the Bible captures something else—it describes the moment John figured it all out. It was when John realized that no one took Jesus away and hid Him. Instead, John knew that Jesus had risen from the dead. Just like He said He would do.

The Bible says, "And he [John] saw and believed" (John 20:8).

Jesus is alive.

Jesus truly is the way, the truth, and the life (John 14:6).

Then Peter and John left the tomb and went home (John 20:10).

I wonder if Peter and John raced home . . . you know, a rematch.

But Mary stayed there, and she was weeping outside the tomb. And when she stooped to look in the tomb, she saw two angels in white sitting where the

Mary didn't know that grace had triumphed over death yet.

body of Jesus had once lain (John 20:11–12). One of the angels was sitting where Jesus' feet were. And the other was sitting where the head of Jesus had been (v. 12). And the angels asked Mary, "Why are you weeping?" (v. 13).

Mary didn't know that grace had triumphed over death yet.

Mary's response to the angels was, "They have taken away my Lord, and I do not know where they have laid him" (v. 13).

In other words, Mary was still grieving that Jesus had to endure the abuse of the cross.

Then Mary turned around and saw someone, *she saw Jesus*, but she didn't know it was Him (v. 14).

This man said to her, "Why are you weeping? Whom are you seeking?"

And Mary said, thinking He was *the gardener*, "Sir, if you have carried him away, tell me where you have laid him, and I will take him away" (v. 15).

Then Jesus said to her, "Mary." And she turned and said to Jesus in Aramaic, "Rabboni!" (John 20:16).

This is the moment when Mary knew that grace had triumphed over sin. That with the resurrection, Jesus has defeated death.

Let's leave the gospel of John for just a second and go to Romans 5.

Here Paul reflects on the power of God's grace in Christ's death, burial, and resurrection.

In order to do this Paul starts by going all the way to the beginning, when Adam and Eve ate from the fruit of the knowledge of good and evil. He writes, "Sin came into the world through one man, and death through sin, and so death spread to all men because all sinned" (Rom. 5:12).

Paul here is talking about the real, lasting effects of the Fall as we discussed early on in Part Two.

God's grace was never intended to condone sin, but He did intend grace to endure our sinfulness, and triumph over it.

Perhaps you are still asking, "Why did it have to be that way?"

The answer is because of what occurred as a result of the Fall.

That because of the Fall, sin entered the world through Adam, and so death spread to all people. Then Paul writes,

> But the free gift is not like the trespass. For if many died through one man's trespass, much more have the grace of God and the free gift by the grace of that one man Jesus Christ abounded for many. And the free gift is not like the result of that one man's sin. For the judgment following one trespass brought condemnation, but the free gift following many trespasses brought justification. For if, because of one man's trespass, death reigned through that one man, much more will those who receive the abundance of grace and the free gift of righteousness reign in life through the one man Jesus Christ. (Rom. 5:15–17)

Hold on, what has abounded for many?

Grace.

Paul says that many have died as a result of Adam's trespass, *but* death is not greater than the grace of God "and the free gift by the grace of that one man Jesus Christ," which has abounded for many (Rom. 5:15).

Then Paul says that those who receive the abundance of grace and the free gift of righteousness will reign in life through Jesus. The reality of reigning in life can only be possible if Jesus reigns in life. And He does, because of the resurrection. In the resurrection, Jesus has triumphed over the abuse of death and provided life for all who believe in Him.

In order to affirm this, Paul says,

> Therefore, as one trespass led to condemnation for all men, so one act of righteousness leads to justification and life for all men. For as by the one man's disobedience the many were made sinners, so by the one man's obedience the many will be made righteous. Now the law came in to increase the trespass, but where sin increased, grace abounded all the more, so that, as sin reigned in death, grace also might reign through righteousness leading to eternal life through Jesus Christ our Lord. (Rom. 5:18–21)

Paul's theology is that due to sin, death reigns. However, in response to death and sin, grace has abounded all the more leading to eternal life through Jesus Christ.

Thus, with the resurrection of Christ death has been defeated.

This sounds wonderful, yet in our world today, death still reigns.

People still die.

The reality is that by God's grace death has already been defeated, ensuring eternal life for all who believe. However, until Jesus returns, and the dead are raised, we will not yet experience the fullness of what Jesus accomplished in His resurrection.

But we have hope. Not a hope in what might happen. But we have an hope anchored in what did happen. A hope that with the resurrection, death is not the end for those who believe in Jesus Christ.

Why?

Because God has graciously defeated death.

Interlude: The Resurrection

As we continue with Part Three, we look at another helpful illustration from the Bible whereby the grace of God triumphs over the effects of sin. This example comes from the promise of our bodily resurrection.

CHAPTER 30

Immortality

Have you ever found yourself struggling with the thought of death? For example, this could be a fear about how you might die. For me, it's always a shark attack.

Or it could be a deep sadness about leaving your loved ones behind.

Maybe there is a fear of the unknown, such as, what will happen when you die? Where will you go? What will you see? What if everything you've believed as a Christian turns out to be wrong?

You're not alone. Asking these questions is normal. Ever since the Fall of mankind, people have been wrestling with our mortality.

In fact, for many in the early church they were sad and confused because when Christians died, nothing different was happening. They were burying their dead just like everyone else. And long after three days in the tomb, their dead weren't coming back to life. It got to the point that some Christians were denying that our bodies would ever rise from the dead. Instead, they believed that only our souls would resurrect from the dead.

In one of Paul's letters he responds to these questions. And the gospel is what forms the basis for his thinking.

That said, what's the gospel?

The gospel isn't a group of words that you repeat that saves you. The gospel isn't just asking Jesus into your heart. The gospel is a belief in the redemptive activity of Jesus Christ. And in 1 Corinthians 15 we have one of our clearest explanations of what the gospel is. Paul writes, "For I delivered to you as of first importance what I also received" (v. 3).

What did Paul receive?

The gospel.

Then he explains what the gospel is: "That Christ died for our sins in accordance with the Scriptures, that he was buried, that he was raised on the third day in accordance with the Scriptures, and that he appeared to Cephas, then to the twelve" (vv. 3–5).

According to Paul, the gospel is that Jesus died for our sins in accordance with the Scriptures (v. 3). That Jesus was buried, and that three days later He rose from the dead in accordance with the Scriptures (v. 4). That's what we believe in our hearts. We believe this to be true.

Then Paul says that after Jesus rose from the dead He appeared to many people; moreover, at the time Paul was writing this, many of these people who saw the resurrected Lord were still alive (v. 6)!

This is the redemptive activity of Jesus Christ.

Not just a spiritual death, burial, and resurrection. But a bodily one as well.

Thus, everything Paul is about to say hinges on the belief in the gospel.

Paul then asks two questions, and both questions directly relate to God's grace triumphing over death.

Here's the first question, verse 12: "Now if Christ is proclaimed as raised from the dead, how can some of you say that there is no resurrection of the dead?" In other words, Paul is saying that this is nonsense. Do you believe in the gospel? If you believe in the gospel, then you believe that Christ rose from the dead. And if you believe that Christ rose from the dead, then you should also believe that Christ will raise you from the dead.

As Christians, our hope rests in Christ, and if Christ didn't rise from the dead, Paul writes, "We [Christians] are of all people most to be pitied" (v. 19).

Then Paul continues, "For as by a man came death, by a man has come also the resurrection of the dead. For as in Adam all die, so also in Christ shall all be made alive" (vv. 21–22). And this is very similar to what we talked about last chapter when Paul said in Romans—"For if, because of one man's trespass, death reigned through that one man, much more will those who receive the abundance of grace and the free gift of righteousness reign in life through the one man Jesus Christ" (Rom. 5:17).

But how will they be made alive?

Through the resurrection.

And the only way you can receive the resurrection is if you receive an abundance of grace.

Thus, what Paul is drawing out for us is that by God's grace He has defeated abuse, and the final abuse to be defeated will be death.

Paul says, "The last enemy to be destroyed is death" (1 Cor. 15:26).

We have this confidence because of the gospel, and the belief that Jesus rose from the dead (1 Cor. 15:4). And if Jesus rose from the dead, that means that you and I will rise from the dead too. Even though we still have to die first.

But here is the sad reality. Even though Jesus has triumphed over death, people will still continue to die. Until Jesus returns, death is coming for us all. It's just a matter of time. No one can avoid it.

> **Certain truths about God have "already" consequences for us now, even though they have "not yet" been totally realized or fulfilled.**

When talking about God we have a helpful expression. It goes like this: "Already, but not yet."

What this expression means is that certain truths about God have "already" consequences for us now, even though they have "not yet" been totally realized or fulfilled.

For example, on the cross, Jesus took upon Himself all of our sin. As Christians, He has totally forgiven us as He became our living sacrifice. This "already" took place and was completed on the cross even though we still sin. And when we sin, we confess our sin to God, and He forgives us (1 John 1:9). Thus, even though we have "already" been forgiven because of Christ's work on the cross, we have "not yet" experienced the total freedom from sin until Jesus returns.

That said, what do we do?

We confess our sin and are restored back to the light of fellowship with God (1 John 1:5–10).

This idea that God's grace has defeated death is another good example of "already, but not yet." This means that even though Christ has "already" triumphed over our sinfulness on the cross, there is still the "not yet" reality that we must wait for Jesus to return in order to finally defeat sin. That is when the last enemy (death) will be destroyed (1 Cor. 15:26).

This is what the people in Corinth were confused about.

Likely because their loved ones were dying and not immediately rising from the dead. As a result, they likely concluded that the resurrection was merely a spiritual resurrection and not a bodily resurrection. But Paul is pointing back to the gospel that he had received and was concluding that if Jesus has risen from the dead, which we believe He did, then we too will rise bodily when Jesus returns.

Then Paul anticipates another question. He writes in 1 Corinthians 15:35, "But someone will ask, 'How are the dead raised? With what kind of body do they come?'"

Great question.

Watch what Paul does next. He uses the word "sown," and this word is another way to describe being buried.

Remember the gospel is that Jesus died, was buried (or sown), and three days later rose from the dead (1 Cor. 15:3–5).

Paul writes, "So is it with the resurrection of the dead. What is sown [buried] is perishable; what is raised is imperishable. It is sown [buried] in dishonor; it is raised in glory. It is sown [buried] in weakness; it is raised in power. It is sown [buried] a natural body; it is raised a spiritual body" (1 Cor. 15:42–44).

Let's think of this in terms of God's grace triumphing over death.

To bury a perishable body is to endure death; to be raised imperishable is to triumph over death.

To be sown in dishonor is to endure death; to be raised in glory is to triumph over death.

To be buried in weakness is to endure death; to be raised in power is to triumph over death.

To bury a natural body is to endure death; to be raised a spiritual body is to triumph over death.

Paul then says that in order to inherit the kingdom of God one must put on the imperishable (1 Cor. 15:53).

But what does it mean to put on something imperishable?

Oliver's favorite TV show right now is *Wild Kratts*. It is a show about the Kratt brothers, Chris and Martin. In each episode the brothers go on fun adventures studying all kinds of animals. It could be any animal. But it never fails—while teaching the kids, for example, about bald eagles, they end up having to rescue an eagle from danger or someone wanting to hurt it.

But in order to save the eagle, they have to become the eagle they are studying. And the way they do that is through their "creature power suits." Which are these special suits they put on that help them become the animal, including their ability to take on all the animal's cool powers.

Well, one day we were watching the show, and Oliver saw a commercial that said you could actually buy one of the Kratt brothers' creature power suits. Oliver said, "Dad! It's only $40.00! I have $5.00 in my room now. I could buy one for me and one for Kaden!"

Lolly and I took note and surprised Oliver with his own creature power suit for his birthday. When he opened it, he was so happy and immediately began to get everything ready. It was like he was preparing to literally teleport to Alaska to study bald eagles.

After he put on his suit, he looked sadly over at Lolly and said, "It's a toy! It's not real!" And he teared up.

This is not how the resurrection works. There will be nothing disappointing about it. In the resurrection, the mortal body will put on immortality (1 Cor. 15:53). Not like Oliver putting on his creature power suit hoping to become a bald eagle. No. We put on immortality. We clothe ourselves with what is imperishable. And in that moment, we will proclaim as fulfilled: "Death is swallowed up in victory. O death, where is your victory? O death, where is your sting?" (Here Paul in 1 Corinthians 15:54–55 is referring to the prophecy in Isaiah 25:8.)

God's grace has triumphed over death. Once again, we have to return to our saying concerning the "already, but not yet."

According to Paul, death has "already" been defeated based on the gospel. When we die we will go be with the Lord immediately (2 Cor. 5:8). However, our bodies will remain in the ground until Jesus returns. Then one day, hopefully soon, when Jesus returns, our souls will be reunited with our now glorified bodies.

This all happens because Jesus died for our sins, was buried, and three days later rose from the dead.

This is the gospel.

Because of His grace enduring our sinfulness on the cross, He has made it possible for us to have life, everlasting life with God. However, we must remain hopeful, because we are "not yet" there.

One last thing—at the beginning of our time we talked about the very first instance of grace in the Bible.

Do you remember where it was?

In was in the very first verse of the Bible, "In the beginning God created."

Then we talked about the first instance of grace after the Fall.

Do you remember when that was?

It was in Genesis 3:20, when God clothed Adam and Eve prior to them leaving the garden. God wanted to graciously clothe them even though Adam and Eve had attempted to clothe themselves with fig leaves.

This idea of clothing is significant to our story about God's grace, because later in the Bible we learn that at our conversion we are justified.

Which means that as a new creation, when the Father looks at us, He no longer sees us but He sees His Son.

But why?

Because we have put on or clothed ourselves with Christ. "For as many of you as were baptized into Christ have put on Christ" (Gal. 3:27). "Put on" here in Greek (*enduō*) means to clothe oneself or wear something. What Paul is saying then in Galatians is that as Christians we have now clothed ourselves with Christ.

Then finally, in the end, when Christ returns and the dead are raised and believers in Christ receive their glorified bodies, we will receive our bodies fit to live with God for eternity. Bodies perfect for eternal life.

How is this possible?

Because we will have, by the grace of God, put on or clothed ourselves with immortality, which is imperishable. This is only possible because God has graciously triumphed over death.

CHAPTER 31

Dents

Have you ever wondered what our glorified bodies will be like? Will we have muscles and not have to work out?

If Jesus died and rose from the dead when he was thirty-three years old, does that mean we will look like we're thirty-three?

Will my stomach in my glorified body give me the ability to eat as much food as I want and not get sick?

Will my brain in my glorified body still learn new things?

Or will I simply wear a white robe and join a heavenly choir singing worship songs to God? Which is totally fine; I just hope my glorified body comes with a better singing voice.

I think these are good questions; however, no one knows. We won't know until it happens. But we can still have fun and wonder and ask, right?

Lolly and I are in a season of life where we don't get to watch much TV. If we do, it's typically something the kids want to watch. And we enjoy that. In fact, Lolly and I always joke that when the kids are grown and gone, they'll still find us watching episodes of *Curious George*.

Nevertheless, after a busy week it is sometimes nice to just snuggle up as a family and watch a movie.

The boys have always loved the *Cars* movies from Disney and Pixar. We've seen them all many times.

The main character in all the *Cars* films is Lightning McQueen. But *Cars 2* is different—the story revolves around Mater. Which is great because he makes us laugh. In *Cars 2*, Lightning and Mater travel to Japan, Italy, and England so that Lightning can compete in the World Grand Prix. However, more than being in a race, Mater ends up getting himself right in the middle of international espionage.

Of course he would.

There is this one scene that gets me every time. Mater is asked to go on a very important mission, but in order to go, he has to put on this suit that allows him to transform into any vehicle as a disguise. However, the suit won't work as long as Mater has all the dents on his body. As a result, Mater's girlfriend (yes, he has a girlfriend) Holley begins to one by one remove all of Mater's dents, scars, and blemishes.

But Mater won't have it.

Mater doesn't want any of his dents to go away. Confused, Holley asks him why. He replies, "Because each dent represents a memory with my best friend."

What could this possibly have to do with the resurrection?

Well, every time I watch this scene I think of our glorified bodies.

Watching Disney movies with me sounds like a blast, right?

After Jesus' resurrection in John 20, Jesus appears to the disciples. Well, all the disciples except Thomas.

Once Thomas finds out the others said they've seen Jesus, he insists, "Unless I see in his hands the mark of the nails, and place my finger into the mark of the nails, and place my hand into his side, I will never believe" (John 20:25–26).

Eight days go by and nothing. Thomas still hasn't seen the resurrected Lord.

Then the disciples were inside, and Thomas was with them (John 20:26). John describes how the doors were locked and yet "Jesus came and stood among them and said, 'Peace be with you'" (v. 26). Then Jesus went to Thomas and told him to "put your finger here, and see my hands; and put out your hand, and place it in my side. Do not disbelieve, but believe" (v. 27).

Then Thomas proclaimed, "My Lord and my God!" (v. 28).

Then Jesus extends grace to Thomas.

You might be thinking, "How so?"

Because of what Jesus does next. He tells Thomas, "Have you believed because you have seen me? Blessed are those who have not seen and yet have believed" (v. 29). The best response from Thomas would have been to simply believe that Jesus had risen. And Jesus affirms this with His charge to Thomas to believe without seeing. However, Jesus still graciously invites Thomas to touch the scars, or in the case of Mater, the dents.

And Jesus' scars tell a gracious story. One in which grace will never endure our sinfulness again because of Jesus' work on the cross. Forevermore, Jesus' body will be a reminder of what grace accomplished on the cross.

That's why we can't miss the small detail that when Jesus received His glorified body, it wasn't a body without those scars. His dents were still there.

What could that mean for us?

Here me out, as I'm fully aware that I could be wrong. But I won't be at all surprised if the remnant of our scars remain and carry over to our glorified bodies. Just like Jesus. Perhaps they are literal scars, or maybe they are emotional or psychological.

But why would they be there?

Because when you and I meet Jesus one day, those scars will serve as an everlasting reminder of what the Lord has done for us. How He was our hope in our most hopeless moments.

We might not be able to tell those stories right now, but one day we will.

In glory, what will be so amazing is that because Jesus is alive, those scars will represent what grace was able to defeat on our behalf.

Wouldn't it be something if one of the ways we worship God in heaven is with our dents, as we tell stories and listen to stories of God's grace dent after dent after dent.

Or maybe we just have the perfect, flawless, thirty-something-year-old body.

Interlude: New Heaven and New Earth

As we continue with Part Three, we find another helpful illustration from the Bible whereby the grace of God triumphs over the effects of sin. This example comes from the promise of the new heaven and new earth.

CHAPTER 32

God with Us

Have you spent much time reading Revelation?

It's an interesting book. And by interesting, I mean it's confusing.

Not only because of what it describes, but it's difficult to figure out what it means. I also think because it can be so "out there" at times, Revelation has been used by a lot of different people to say a lot of different things about God. And because of that, I wonder if Revelation has been given an unfair reputation as "weird" or "scary."

However, I hope that changes a little as we spend time together in this amazing book of the Bible.

Moreover, just because it is confusing doesn't mean we should avoid it. If we skipped all the things confusing about God, we wouldn't end up spending much time with Him. Instead, we should try our best to figure out what it says.

Revelation was written by John, the disciple whom Jesus loved (John 20:2).

The same John who wrote four other books in the Bible (gospel of John, 1–3 John).

The same John whom Jesus told from the cross to take care of His mom (John 19:27).

The same John who beat Peter to Jesus' tomb (John 20:4).

The same John who saw the resurrected Lord (John 21:24).

And this was John's final letter.

Right at the beginning, John writes,

The revelation of Jesus Christ, which God gave him to show to his servants the things that must soon take place. He made it known by sending his angel to his servant John, who bore witness to the word of God and to the testimony of Jesus Christ, even to all that he saw. Blessed is the one who reads aloud the words of this prophecy, and blessed are those who hear, and who keep what is written in it, for the time is near. (Rev. 1:1–3)

John postures the heart of the reader to be ready. There is an urgency that what he is writing will take place soon.

But when will soon be (Rev. 1:1)?

We don't know.

No one knows.

Then John explains that this vision that he received was so important that God sent an angel to help him interpret the vision (vv. 1–2). Remember, John has written other books in the Bible, but this one was different. Writing this one came with the help of an angel.

It's also intriguing that this book in the Bible describes that if you read it aloud, you will be blessed. John writes, "Blessed is the one who reads aloud the words of this prophecy" (v. 3). Obviously, reading any book of the Bible would be a blessing, but it is interesting that this book goes out of its way to explain the one who reads it aloud will be blessed.

It is here in Revelation that we will discover God's grace finally defeating sin. It is no longer the "already, but not yet." What we find in the book of Revelation is that it is done. And specifically we will see this with the last two chapters of Revelation, which also happen to be the last two chapters in the Bible.

We have really covered some ground.

Remember when we started our journey how we spent all that time in the first few chapters of Genesis? Now we will finish our time together in the last few chapters of Revelation.

From the beginning I've tried to reveal that grace is so much more than something that saves you. That without God's grace, a relationship with God is not possible. That means prior to the Fall it was grace that was providing the neces-

> **This is humbling, that the triune God would pursue us.**

sary conditions for us to dwell with God. Then after the Fall, it was grace again, but this time grace was enduring our sinfulness so that we might have a relationship with God. And in the new heaven and new earth, it will be grace once again that will provide the necessary conditions for us to have an everlasting relationship with God.

This is humbling, that the triune God would pursue us like this.

And let's not forget, that while grace was holding together our relationship with God throughout humanity's story, grace never changed. By God's design and plan, at each stage of human history we have come to learn more and more about who God is and the grace He has given us as our story continues to unfold.

You ready?

In Revelation 21, John receives a vision in which he sees a new heaven and a new earth. He describes how the "first heaven and the first earth had passed away, and the sea was no more" (v. 1).

Then John writes, "And I saw the holy city, new Jerusalem, coming down out of heaven from God, prepared as a bride adorned for her husband" (v. 2). What we find here is intimate relational language as the new Jerusalem is like a bride adorned for her husband.

Then John recounts how a loud voice from the throne said, "Behold, the dwelling place of God is with man. He will dwell with them, and they will be his people, and God himself will be with them as their God" (v. 3). The mysterious relational language continues, but as it unfolds it is getting more and more specific.

John describes "a bride adorned for her husband" (Rev. 21:2).

Who is the bride?

The bride is the church (Eph. 5:22–33).

And the church is brought near to God. The bride is to dwell with the groom. Where sin had forced the bride and groom to be apart, now in the new heaven and the new earth, they are together again.

When God joins something together, it is not meant to be separated.

God and humans will now dwell together. Forever.

One thing that always happens when God dwells with us is that God comes down to us. He always meets us right where we are.

A helpful example of this comes from Philippians 2:5–11. Paul writes,

> Have this mind among yourselves, which is yours in Christ Jesus, who, though he was in the form of God, did not count equality with God a thing to be grasped, but emptied himself, by taking the form of a servant, being born in the likeness of men. And being found in human form, he humbled himself by becoming obedient to the point of death, even death on a cross. Therefore God has highly exalted him and bestowed on him the name that is above every name, so that at the name of Jesus every knee should bow, in heaven and on earth and under the earth, and every tongue confess that Jesus Christ is Lord, to the glory of God the Father.

Here Paul is talking about the supernatural moment when Christ left the right hand of the Father and added to Himself full humanity in order to endure the cross so that we, as sinners, might have a relationship with God. But in order to accomplish this for eternity, Jesus left His rightful place on the throne, and He came down to us.

In Revelation it is happening again. God is choosing to dwell with these creatures created in His image (Rev. 21:3). Things changed after the Fall, and dwelling with God looked different. It had too. But we can't forget that everything was always pointing to this moment when God would permanently dwell with humanity. And for John, these "things must soon take place" (Rev. 1:1).

Then John writes, "He will wipe away every tear from their eyes, and death shall be no more, neither shall there be morning, nor crying, nor pain anymore, for the former things have passed away" (Rev. 21:4). God is bringing forth the new Jerusalem for the purpose of having a relationship with us. He is making the pronouncement that He desires to be with us.

But how is that possible?

Because He has graciously triumphed over sin.

And when sin is defeated, you are able to finally wipe away every tear from your eyes.

You are able to say death shall be no more.

You are able to say that mourning shall be no more.

You are able to say that crying will be no more.

You are able to say pain is no more.

Why?

Because God says, "For the former things have passed away" (Rev. 21:4).

But how?

Because grace has triumphed over sin.

CHAPTER 33

It Is Done!

I t wasn't too long ago that we talked about the resurrection of Jesus. About how Jesus rose from the dead, and because He defeated death, we too have hope in the gospel that we will rise from the dead one day. When we will no longer suffer from any of the effects of the Fall.

However, this doesn't change our condition right now.

In theology we have a term that helps us wrap our minds around this idea. It's called total depravity, which means that after the Fall, humankind is totally and completely affected by sin nature.

This is why humans do sinful things (Rom. 3:23). This is also why humans can't help but do sinful things (Rom. 7:15). This is why God's grace was never intended to condone sin, but He did design grace to endure our sinfulness, and triumph over it.

And get this—no one is immune to the damaging effects of the Fall. No one is able to avoid this condition after the Fall. This is why Paul writes, "Therefore, just as sin came into the world through one man, and death through sin, and so death spread to all men because all sinned" (Rom. 5:12).

Thus, it isn't just our behavior that is "sinful"; rather we are completely corrupted by a sin nature. Which is most clearly evident by the fact that one day we all will die.

However, we weren't meant to suffer from total depravity. We were never meant to die.

You might be thinking, "How can you be so sure?"

Let's get back to Revelation 21 as John continues to record what he hears from the one seated on the throne. "Behold, I am making all things new" (v. 5).

This time, instead of our glorified bodies, now Jesus is talking about the new heaven and the new earth. The dwelling place for mankind will be restored and given life apart from the Fall.

A few verses earlier, God had said that He will dwell with His people (Rev. 21:3). But in order for God to be with them, like He lived with them in the garden, He will need to make all things new.

However, just like our glorified bodies, the new heaven and the new earth will not be something totally different. Instead, God re-creates *this* earth. Remember, what God originally created was good. Very good.

Thus, improving on what God had originally created is not necessary.

Now, you might be thinking, *How long will we live in the new heaven and the new earth?*

How long will we have these glorified bodies?

How long will God dwell with us?

The answer: forever.

But how do I know this?

Because in the next verse God proclaims from the throne, "It is done!" (Rev. 21:6).

What is done?

You remember how on the seventh day of creation God rested.

What did He rest from?

He rested from "his work that he had done" (Gen. 2:2).

Notice all the times the word "done" is mentioned on the seventh day: "God finished his work that he had *done*, and he rested on the seventh day from all his work that he had *done*. So God blessed the seventh day and made it holy, because on it God rested from all his work that he had *done* in creation" (Gen. 2:2–3).

You remember how the seventh day was unique in the creation account because this particular day had no end. All the other days of creation ended with "And there was evening and there was morning," but on the seventh day it doesn't mention this. Thus, we concluded that the seventh day is still unfolding.

God resting with and within His creation was never meant to end.

Today, in order for creatures created in God's image to rest with God in a fallen world, grace would have to endure our sinfulness for a time. But in the end, God also knew grace would triumph over sin and provide the necessary conditions for us to rest with God forever.

Now I hope you will forgive me, but I forgot to mention something back in Part One about the word "rest." Remember what Genesis 2:2 says? "And on the seventh day God finished his work that he had done, and he *rested* on the seventh day from all his work that he had done."

The word "rest" (*shevet*) from Genesis 2:1–3 also means "dwell."

Which means that God not only "finished his work that he had done" on the seventh day, but that God willingly chose to dwell with His creation. Thus, we are most at rest when we are dwelling with God.

In other words, the biblical story from beginning to end is a story of God's pursuit of us. God's desire to rest with us. God's plan to dwell with us.

Back to our earlier question in this chapter: "What is done?"

John records that the one seated on the throne said, "It is done! I am the Alpha and the Omega, the beginning and the end" (Rev. 21:6).

The announcement that "It is done" is God's way of declaring that grace has triumphed. And instead of the creation account from Genesis, that a mere day has begun and ended, now the "Alpha and Omega, the beginning and the end" is saying, "It is done!"

Which means we will now rest with God forever. We will now dwell with God forever.

God is done being separated from His creation and mankind who were created in His image.

The days of God and His children not dwelling together are over.

Now, forever, God will dwell with and within His creation.

God has moved into their neighborhood forever.

CHAPTER 34

What If We Sin Again?

Have you ever wondered what would happen if, in the new heaven and the new earth, someone sins again? Would that mean we'd have to go through the Fall again? Would grace have to endure our sinfulness all over again?

Have you ever thought about that?

You might be thinking, *Well, no. But now you just ruined my day.*

Back in chapter 9 we mentioned this, but I told you that we had to wait until Part Three to discuss it more. Well, now is that time.

Right after giving an account of the new heaven and the new earth, John describes being carried away in the Spirit "to a great, high mountain" and there being shown the new "holy city Jerusalem coming down out of heaven from God" (Rev. 21:10).

This is what he saw.

Its radiance like a most rare jewel, like a jasper, clear as crystal. It had a great, high wall, with twelve gates, and at the gate twelve angels, and on the gates the names of the twelve tribes of the sons of Israel were inscribed—on the east three gates, on the north three gates, on the south three gates, and on the west three gates. And the wall of the city had twelve foundations, and on them were the twelve names of the twelve apostles of the Lamb. (Rev. 21:11–14)

Then as John gives details of the shape of the new Jerusalem, he writes, "And the one who spoke with me had a measuring rod of gold to measure the city and its gates and walls. The city lies foursquare, its length the same as its width" (vv. 15–16).

Wait, so the new Jerusalem is a box?

I thought we weren't supposed to put God in a box.

Dad joke. Sorry.

After he describes that the city is made of the most precious and rare jewels, John then makes an interesting observation. He notices that there is no temple in the new Jerusalem (v. 22).

Because Jesus Himself is with us, there is no need for the temple.

Why would there be no temple?

John explains—and remember he is seeing this with his own eyes—that this is because the temple of the new Jerusalem is Jesus Himself. God is dwelling with us.

He writes, "And I saw no temple in the city, for its temple is the Lord God the Almighty and the Lamb" (v. 22).

He is dwelling with us.

And because Jesus Himself is with us, there is no need for the temple.

Instead of having a secluded place called the holy of holies where God dwells in the temple, now the new Jerusalem *is* the holy of holies. We will be living *in* the holy of holies *in* God's presence.

Then John describes something else about the new Jerusalem. He says that in the new Jerusalem "nothing unclean will ever enter it, nor anyone who does what is detestable or false, but only those who are written in the Lamb's book of life" (v. 27).

There isn't any question or doubt or hesitation in John. He isn't saying there *might be*, or *if* anyone detestable enters.

No.

He says emphatically, nothing unclean will *ever* enter the new Jerusalem.

Then he goes on to explain that the angel showed him the river of the water of life (Rev. 22:1). This river was "bright as crystal," and flowed from the throne of God through the middle of the street of the new Jerusalem (vv. 1–2). It also says that on either side of the river of life is the tree of life (v. 2). And the tree of life was ripe with fruit. John explains how it had twelve kinds of fruit and that it yielded its fruit each month (v. 2).

Remember that Adam and Eve ate the fruit from the tree of the knowledge of good and evil.

They sinned.

And as a result, everything changes.

Prior to the Fall they were able to eat from "every tree of the garden," which would have included the tree of life (Gen. 2:16). However, after the Fall, God specifically explains why he is removing them from the garden.

He says, "'Behold, the man has become like one of us in knowing good and evil. Now, lest he reach out his hand and take also of the tree of life and eat, and live forever—' therefore the LORD God sent him out from the garden of Eden to work the ground from which he was taken" (Gen. 3:22–23). God even placed the cherubim and a flaming sword that turned every way to guard the tree of life (v. 24).

God was not going to allow Adam and Eve to eat from the tree of life in their fallen, sinful condition.

Why?

Because eating from the tree of life in their fallen condition would mean they would live forever in that fallen condition. And that wasn't God's plan. He had other ideas. And God's grace was always the means to accomplishing that plan.

Back to Revelation.

Did you know that from Revelation 21:9 to Revelation 22:5 there is no longer any mention of the tree of the knowledge of good and evil? There is no longer any mention of the cherubim and a flaming sword protecting the tree of life. Instead, because God knows the Fall will never happen again, He graciously provides the fruit of the tree of life. We will eat this fruit without any limitation once again. As it was supposed to be.

But we can't forget why.

God sovereignly knew in the beginning that the Fall would occur. But just as God knew the Fall would occur, God also knows that the Fall won't occur in the new heaven and the new earth.

That is why Jesus proclaims, "It is done!"

CHAPTER 35

Come Lord Jesus!

J esus is coming soon (Rev. 22:6–21).

This is something we believe as Christians.

That's why John said at the beginning of his letter, "The revelation of Jesus Christ, which God gave him to show to his servants the things that must soon take place" (Rev. 1:1).

Then he ends his letter with, "These words are trustworthy and true. And the Lord, the God of the spirits of the prophets, has sent his angel to show his servants what must soon take place" (Rev. 22:6).

John ends just how he began, imploring the reader to believe that Jesus will soon return.

That John's words are "trustworthy" and "true."

Reminds me of "Jonah the son of Amittai." Or we could say, "God's beloved dove, the son of truth."

Reminds me of Pilate asking Jesus, "What is truth?"

Yes, these words are trustworthy and true. And they tell a gracious story about God's unwavering, relentless love for us.

But the question becomes, do you believe they are true?

Ultimately, that's for you to wrestle with and answer for yourself.

As you ponder this, I have a question for you—do you pray for Jesus to return?

Your answer to this question might reveal how truthful you believe these words to be.

Your answer might reveal just how much you think grace will triumph in the end.

As Christians we want Jesus to return, but typically we want Jesus to return after we experience some milestone or an event in our life.

For example, I want Jesus to return, but I *really* want to get married first, then He can return.

I want Jesus to return, but I *really* want to travel and see the world first.

I want Jesus to return, but I *really* want to succeed in my career first.

But what are we *really* saying?

Not in a malicious way, but what we are communicating in that moment is that we are okay with the conditions of this fallen world and the brokenness of our relationship with God. So much so that we are willing to delay the return of Jesus when all things will be made new (Rev. 21:5). When grace will finally triumph over our sinfulness.

Sin has this effect on us.

It normalizes what would otherwise be a dysfunctional environment . . . until the dysfunction hits too close to home.

I remember how dysfunctional it was when my parents first got a divorce. My parents tried their hardest to make things "normal." And in many ways, they did a great job. But no matter how much effort goes into it, that first Christmas is still weird. It doesn't matter if you celebrate Christmas twice and get double the presents. Or if somehow both parents agree to celebrate Christmas together "for the kids."

Either way, it's dysfunctional.

But what happens over time?

The second Christmas, then the third, then the fourth, what happens?

You almost stop thinking about it.

It just becomes Christmas.

But what has changed?

Nothing.

Your parents are still divorced. New family traditions have been made. And whether we are aware of it or not, we have just grown comfortable with the dysfunction. This is what sin nature does. This is what living in a fallen world does. We grow comfortable with grace enduring our sinfulness.

What then should be our response to this fallen world?

It should be a greater desire for Jesus to return. It should be for Jesus to come back right now.

Why?

So that we might enjoy the rest we were intended for from the beginning. So that we might dwell with God. So that our relationship with God might be restored to the way it was supposed to be. Which was perfect and complete. Lacking in nothing.

Christians who truly believe that God's grace has triumphed over sin, say, "Come, Lord Jesus! The grace of the Lord Jesus be with all. Amen" (Rev. 22:20–21).

CHAPTER 36

Grace Beyond Salvation

We have been on quite a journey.

And we have covered a lot of ground.

We began in the first verse of the Bible and ended with the last.

Along the way we have stopped and explored both the Old and New Testaments, looking at what grace has accomplished through the lives of Adam and Eve, Jonah, the Prodigal Son, and Jesus.

What we discovered is that grace is so much more than something that saves you. That God's grace was never intended to condone sin, but He did design grace to endure our sinfulness, and triumph over it. And as we have seen in the story of God's grace, this was always in the context of something He has endured for us.

Not something God expects us to endure.

This was most clearly evidenced by the cross.

Moreover, that God's grace would endure our sinfulness is only a part of the story of God's grace. It wasn't the way things were supposed to be. And one day, God's grace will triumph once and for all.

But in the meantime, to truly embrace the breadth of our relationship with God, we can't avoid the fallen reality that if sinners are going to dwell with God, then grace must endure our sinfulness.

This is how God demonstrates His grace.

This was His plan.

Not ours.

Full disclosure—while writing this book I often found myself wrestling with insecurity.

Unpacking the enormity of the biblical story of God's grace is a tall order and, to be honest, there were times when I wasn't sure if I could do it. But I also felt a conviction; it was as though by not retelling this story I would have been disobeying God. Not because He was dependent on me to write this book; rather, I think God wanted to show me something.

This journey was just as important for me as it was for you.

On top of that, there have been many other books written on grace. What could I possibly contribute that hasn't already been said? However, the more I prayed, the more I realized God wasn't actually putting any pressure on me to uncover something new about grace. The Lord had already revealed the story He wanted me to tell. It was *His* gracious story. Conveyed through His Word.

My purpose was to merely show you the way.

I wanted you to see the story as God had laid it out. A story about Jesus you never knew always existed from Genesis to Revelation. The story of the grace of the Lord Jesus.

I'm thankful you joined me.

Remember, I told you where we are going is a safe and loving and hopeful place. It's a place where God is. And where God can be found. It's where we dwell with God.

Now that you know the way, I want you to know that you can go back as often as you'd like.

And my hope is that you will show others how to get there too.

Acknowledgments

As I sit with the reality that this book is done, I'm thankful. Thankful for the graciousness of God at every step of the way.

I'm thankful for my church (Scottsdale Bible Church), specifically Michelle Clifford—thank you for creating the space and time each year to be creative and write.

To my students at Arizona Christian University. You are amazing. Getting to be your professor is a privilege. Thank you for always entertaining my crazy ideas long before I start writing. Those moments in the classroom helped form what later became these words.

Pam Pugh, what a gift you've been. You are a true professional and editorial wizard. From the start you understood not just me but what this book was trying to accomplish. You made this book better and I'm thankful for your friendship.

Trillia Newbell, thank you (and Moody Publishers) for believing in me. Weaving the story of God's grace throughout this book was not easy. But I never felt alone. I often think back to those early theological conversations and how necessary they were. By God's grace, I think we did it. Thank you for partnering with me; it's been a joy.

Teresa Evenson, you are not just my agent, but my friend. What a gift you are. You love and shepherd your authors so well. I'll forever be grateful that you believe in me.

Mom and Dad, thank you for your unwavering love and support. It truly is a gift. I love you.

Lolly, you have taught me more about grace than anyone else. Because of the way you love your friends, family, the boys (Kaden, Oliver, and Carson), and me, we all know just a little more about what it means to be gracious. Besides Jesus, you are God's greatest gift to me. Every single day you extend grace to me, and I am better for it. It makes me want to follow Jesus more. I love you.

You finished reading!

Did this book help you in some way? If so, please consider writing an honest review wherever you purchase your books. Your review gets this book into the hands of more readers and helps us continue to create biblically faithful resources.

Moody Publishers books help fund the training of students for ministry around the world.

The **Moody Bible Institute** is one of the most well-known Christian institutions in the world, training thousands of young people to faithfully serve Christ wherever He calls them. And when you buy and read a book from Moody Publishers, you're helping make that vital ministry training possible.

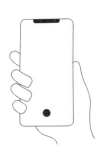

Continue to dive into the Word, *anytime, anywhere.*

Find what you need to take your next step in your walk with Christ: from uplifting music to sound preaching, our programs are designed to help you right when you need it.

Download the **Moody Radio App** and start listening today!

 MOODY Publishers

 MOODY Bible Institute

 MOODY Radio